THE TEA LEAF PARADOX

PARADOX

(Discovering Beer in
the Land of Whisky)

Robert Middleton

To all beer lovers everywhere

Table of Contents

1 Campervan for Real Ale

"He's got a turbo? Really?" This was my shocked response upon
hearing the news that our recently imported, 1988 VW campervan had
a high performance accessory hidden within his very low performance
engine. Less surprising was the news that it was broken. Coming on
top of an earlier discovery that his engine was not 1.9 litres as we had
been led to believe, but a miserly 1.6, it was all beginning to make
sense. For the last three months while driving through Europe we had
shaped our route so as to avoid anything resembling a hill, never mind
a mountain. Approaching an incline felt a little like walking toward
the dentist's chair - you knew it was going to be painful, but you knew
it had to be done. My heart would sink in sync with the speedometer
needle as our spirits dropped with the gears. Shifting any gear required
a fine balance of brute force and manual dexterity. Locating the right
gear involved a degree of luck, but that loud crunching noise at least
confirmed that you'd found 3rd. It was embarrassing, a little dangerous
and would send the engine temperature soaring relentlessly toward the
red zone. Stopping to let him cool down was both sensible and
possible (as his brakes worked fine when going uphill) but remaining
stopped was harder as the handbrake was losing its grip, as were we.
Besides the mechanical challenges, it had taken us weeks to figure out
how the internal electrics worked, by which time we had blown the
fuses across an entire Belgian campsite and didn't even seem able to

boil a kettle without tripping a circuit.

So why did we decide to import this ageing wreck? Love! We had fallen in love with our van, as you do when sharing adventure and adversity together. We knew that we could probably buy a new one for what the repairs were going to cost but couldn't bear to part with our Brian. Yes, Brian. So named because his age, colour and snail-like speed reminded us of the character from the Magic Roundabout. One could best describe his body colour as sludge brown, capped by an off-white roof that is tall enough to allow one to stand up inside but prohibits the use of indoor and multi-storey car parks. This colour scheme does give him the overall look of a cappuccino on wheels but he wears it well. His quirks are many – such as headlights that are almost uselessly dim and a wing mirror that collapses in a strong breeze. Being originally Dutch (we found him in Utrecht), he is blessed with the endearing twist of being left-hand drive. I would love to tell you that he's pretty on the inside but unfortunately this is not the case. The general state of decoration is best described as 'neglected 70's', the roof space is unsuitable for human habitation, the curtains don't close properly, the tap's floppy, the sink's blocked and, try as we might, there's a constant essence of damp. So yep, love!

We had already decided on a new clutch and gear box before hearing the troubling turbo news but, given our previous experiences, it was a 'no-brainer' to decide to pop a new turbo in there too. Just for good measure (and to get his roadworthiness certificate, or 'MoT') we also fixed his brakes (foot and hand), sorted the mirror, fitted new lights fit for purpose on Britain's highways and installed a fresh pair of wipers. We only just avoided having to replace his kph speedo with an mph one thanks to a little loophole between the law and what's required to get an MoT certificate. (If the reader is a DVLA (Vehicle Licensing) employee, then please ignore that last sentence.) So, several thousand pounds and one month after entering Blighty for the first time, Brian was now in his best condition for years and was proudly displaying his new registration plates. He was still sludge brown, but he was British!

Those three months in Europe marked the end of a two-year break from reality, travelling the world with my partner Jo. We managed to spin the good times out a bit longer, working as Olympic volunteers and hanging out at music festivals, but the time had come to settle back down to life in London. Having walked away from the high-octane world of occupational pensions two years earlier I certainly had no wish to return but also realised that I didn't possess any other employable skills! Where would I find a new purpose in life? I considered everything from tutoring maths to training as an electrician (a terrible idea given the calamity mentioned above) but nothing really appealed. I'd kept a blog while we were away so maybe there was a way I could continue to travel and carry on writing? Various ideas were conjured up then discarded such as: touring all the best gig venues in Europe, searching for rare Eastern European cheeses and a project called 'Hitched' where I would take hitchhikers wherever they wanted to go and see where I ended up. Then, as often happens, inspiration arrived when least expected.

I had just finished reading Iain Banks' book, 'Raw Spirit', about his journey around Scotland visiting several distilleries and indulging his love of whisky, Scotland and driving. This seemed like tremendous fun but he'd already done the whisky thing and there aren't many wineries in Scotland, so what about beer? As a recent convert to real ale I had been missing a good pint of warm, fizz-less beer for the last couple of years, there was so much of Scotland I hadn't yet seen and now I had a campervan, all souped-up and ready for a road trip. Like most people I strongly associated Scotland with whisky, not real ale. Indeed, the only 'brew' that Scotland has been well known for is Irn Bru, a fizzy drink 'made from girders' as one advertising campaign claimed. Real 'ale' was something I associated with England, village pubs, old men, folk music, chunky sweaters and serious beards. Actually, come to think about it, I live in England, I'm definitely getting old and I quite like pubs and folk music. I'm just a sweater and a beard away from the whole ticket!

So, I had found my purpose, my quest – to journey with Brian through Scotland to discover the world of beer, especially real ales, in the land of whisky. I had some questions to be answered: What exactly is *real* ale? Does it have to be 'real' to be really good? How does Scottish real ale compare to the traditional English pint? My research had revealed that there were something like 60 or 70 independent breweries in Scotland, spread from the Shetlands to the Borders, the Highlands to the Lowlands and the cities to the isles. These ranged from the big players (Caledonian, Belhaven) to the small fry (anything from post redundancy cheque dreamers to smart, fresh graduates), and the old school (Traquair, Broughton) to the new kids on the block (most dramatically led by BrewDog, the fast-growing craft beer evangelists).

At this stage I had never before been to a brewery and certainly didn't appreciate the subtle differences between real ale and craft beer or the distinction between casks and kegs. One distinction I did appreciate however is that while Scotland has only 10% of England's population, it is 60% of its size. These statistics in combination meant that I had several months of driving through stunning countryside ahead of me, in an old Dutch campervan, visiting as many breweries as possible. Well, someone has to do it! Among my prey there was one brewery in particular that had been a catalyst to accepting this most testing of missions. This quote comes from the Colonsay Brewery website and neatly paints the picture: "Colonsay is the smallest island in the entire world with its own brewery. We employ ten per cent of the island's working population - Chris and Bob." I could already sense the adventure in the air and the heady cocktail of diesel and beer in my nostrils.

So, now I knew what I was doing without being entirely sure about why. I had a couple of weeks of planning ahead to figure out 'how', before hitting the road. First of all I needed some kind of strategy for the route. With winter approaching, the weather was only going to get worse so it made sense to start at the top (north) and work down, getting some of the longer/nastier ferry crossings under my belt on the way. This would mean that my first port of call would be the Valhalla Brewery on the Shetland Isles. Not just any Shetland Isle but actually the most northerly of the 16 inhabited islands, Unst. This launched me into some feverish research to come up with travel logistics that would allow me to get to Shetland then travel down through Orkney before re-joining the mainland. The key to solving this conundrum lay in making the optimal selection from the limited number of ferry crossings each day. After many happy hours of reviewing the options and some in-depth actuarial analysis, I settled on the perfect itinerary. Perfect except my chosen ferry from Aberdeen to Lerwick (Shetland's capital) was full that evening. "One moment", said the young lady on the call, "and I'll see if the boys in freight can shift one o' their trucks oot ra way". Five tense minutes later she returned to confirm that one final space had indeed been made for Brian and five minutes after that our ferries were all booked up.

Unlike nearly every distillery in Scotland, most breweries do not cater for visitors, far less have a proper, functioning visitor centre. This would mean that I would have to rely on the brewers themselves having the time, inclination and courtesy to take time out from making a brew in a vat to chewing the fat. What would the typical brewer be like? What if they were aloof or unfriendly, monosyllabic or incoherent? Why would these busy chaps bother to give me the time of day, far less a guided tour? Let's be clear that while I enjoy a beer as much as the next person, I knew little if anything about what went into it, how it was created and what all the different types were. I would be gaining my education on the road, through the kindness and experience of the brewers I would be meeting. Many of the breweries on my target list are run by just one or two people, some don't even open every day and more than a few are quite hard to find. Well, it would be boring if it were easy. Luckily I had come across a website (www.quaffale.org.uk) that helpfully showed a map of all the breweries in the UK with links to further information and websites. Although I later discovered that this map was missing a few breweries it gave me the start I needed to capture notes, make plans, contact brewers and develop something resembling an itinerary. As the great bard Rabbie Burns once said though "the best laid plans of mice and men gang aft agley".

Next up I had to prepare for the journey. Brian was by now in decent mechanical fettle, even if his paintwork needed some attention and his interior decoration still left a lot to be desired. At least the electrics mostly functioned and he was fairly watertight for his age. My anticipation and excitement peaked when the time came to start packing all the stuff I would need for the months ahead. This mostly involved all manner of clothing garments required to protect against the cold and wet, including a big pair of wellies for nocturnal meanderings in inclement weather, among other uses. Less essential but nonetheless valuable items included supplies of Werther's Originals (or 'travel sweeties' as my parents used to call them), some favourite CDs, a slightly out of date and unpredictable GPS navigation device and series 1-7 of the classic sitcom Only Fools and Horses on DVD; I was expecting some long, cold, lonely evenings. My plan was to sleep in Brian as often as possible to save money, but also to experience some of Scotland's more remote campsites along the way. I knew how cold it may become so was prepared with both quilt and sleeping bag as well as my new thermal beany. I also had a brand new body board with me although I have no idea why. I had planned my route, booked my ferry berth, arranged various forms of accommodation and made tenuous appointments with my first few breweries. The scene was set for the voyage of discovery that lay ahead.

2 Nine Degrees North

The journey begins in Islington, north London, on a dull Sunday morning in late September and I'm all set to load my bags into Brian and head off. Emotionally, I'm feeling a mix of "why am I even doing this" and "woo hoo, a road trip to Scotland with Brian". It certainly feels strange as I make my final preparations but this journey north will be a memorable experience, a step into the unknown, the start of an adventure and my first time ever visiting Shetland. I won't get there until two days from now so I resolve to make the most of my trip from Britain's capital in the south to its most northerly limits, with roughly nine degrees of latitude separating the two. I'd already given Brian a good clean the day before as well as making sure all of his critical fluids were fully topped up. A final look around, outside and in, confirms that everything is in place and ready for take-off. I make some final adjustments to the mirrors, select some CDs, programme my navigation device for Scotland and gently pull away.

It takes a while, even on a Sunday, to escape the confines of London and gather some pace toward our destination. The journey north is anything but scenic as I take the most obvious route past Coventry, Birmingham and Stoke, sandwiched between endless grey motorway and a panoply of grey sky. I am grateful for the lack of rain and wind however and Brian seems to be performing very efficiently at a steady 100kph (sounds so much better than 60 mph). I'm also coping pretty well with driving a left hand drive vehicle on the left hand side of the road. Accurate offside mirror positioning (without any inconvenient bending in the wind) is critically important for safe manoeuvring, but if I twist my head around then my view is aided by Brian having windows all down his right side. That said the real test would come when trying to overtake on twisty country roads in the unlikely event that we come up behind a vehicle going more slowly than Brian. I must say though that the new turbo is transforming my driving experience and pushing us up all but the most challenging of hills. Third gear is slotting in nicely and I have discovered that the CD player is loud enough to drown out the noise of the engine, which seems to be constantly begging for a fifth gear that just doesn't exist. The miles fly by with only the occasional fuel/pee/food stop to punctuate our journey and I'm happily indulging myself with the sounds of Primal Scream, Pixies, Kills and Sleater-Kinney.

My aim on this first day is simply to escape England for the land of whisky before resting ahead of the second leg through Scotland to catch the ferry. My spirits lift as we near the land of my birth and indeed the auspices seem favourable as the sun pops out just ahead of crossing the border into Scotland. Our destination is the Hoddom Castle Camping and Caravanning Park, near Lockerbie. As soon as we cross the border, Gretna Green is signposted to our left. This small village is of course famous for having been the first port of call for young lovers escaping the clutches of their parents' intransigence and eloping over a blacksmith's anvil. Back in the day you could marry in

Scotland at 14 (for boys) and just 12 for girls, without parental consent. The law today of course requires both parties to be 16 but parental consent still applies in England up to age 18, with no such restriction for rebellious, romantic young Scots. Such is the romantic allure of this place that even today something in excess of 5,000 couples still choose it as the ideal place to tie the knot every year and I read that, bizarrely, it's still the venue for one in six marriages in Scotland! I wonder how many people getting married over an anvil end up getting divorced over a barrel?

You know you're in Scotland when the first village you pass through after exiting the motorway has a name like Ecclefechan. It sounds like it could be an excellent blasphemous adjective – 'you're such an Ecclefechan idiot!' Certainly not a name to attempt before swallowing the remains of that partially masticated fish supper you may have been devouring. Carrying on, we quickly find ourselves gliding along the long driveway that leads to the campsite, with the eponymous castle at its centre. It's quite a lovely place, only £14.50 a night and, as I later discovered, just £3 for a pint of Guinness. I park Brian up on his hard-standing pitch and take a short walk round by the twinkling Annan river before the sun leaves the sky. The 325-mile journey has taken a mere 8 hours including stops, which is very respectable for Brian for whom anything over 60 is virtually warp speed. It's my first night away from home and I realise that it's also the first time that I have camped alone in Brian. I feel the prickly pressure of ensuring I don't lock myself out, leave the gas on or fail to close all the windows before retiring. After triple checking everything and a couple of pints of Guinness, I settle down in Brian to consume the spinach and ricotta cannelloni that I've brought from home, washed down with a couple of mini bottles of a fairly decent red wine. Three episodes of Only Fools and Horses later and I'm ready for sleep.

Sleeping in Brian is pretty comfortable but it rained in the night and I had to twice suffer the long, dark walk to the gentlemen's (inconvenient) convenience. This is one of the less attractive parts of camping although the newer, bigger mobile homes seem to all be well equipped with inside facilities. The disadvantage of this apparent luxury is that they do then have to take the container and empty it, which can't be very pleasant after a serious curry. I did consider a potty though and my dad helpfully recommended a large (empty) coffee jar as a cheap and practical solution. I can't quite bring myself to pee in Brian (or a coffee jar for that matter) so the nocturnal meanderings will continue for some time to come.

The news this morning carries stories of severe flood warnings down south, eclipsing our minor, overnight rainfall. It strikes me that we have just passed the autumn equinox, which may not be the best time of year for starting a tour around Scotland. In fact it's probably 6 months out from the ideal timing. However, they do say that Scotland only has two seasons - June and winter - and it can snow in June, so best just to get on with it. I also learned from the bloke at the campsite that my gas bottle, being Dutch, is incompatible with British gas connectors and therefore when it runs out I shall have to replace the whole thing – gas, bottle and regulator. I decide that this is one bridge that I shall cross when we reach it and file the problem under 'pending'. Having executed my breakfast and ablution duties we're soon on the way and seem to be just about keeping ahead of the weather, but the fringes of the storm test out Brian's new wipers as we drive toward Aberdeen to catch the night ferry to Shetland. The route takes me within half a mile of my parents' house in Dundee so I pop in for lunch and a chat and to introduce them to Brian. They must have been expecting a moth-eaten rust bucket as, while Brian's in reasonable nick for his age, being described as 'beautiful' definitely brought some colour to his cheeks. Wherever they are....

After a most welcome pizza and a couple of hours rest, we commence the final leg of the journey to Aberdeen where our ride to Shetland awaits. We reach the ferry in plenty of time and I approach the check in gate, ready to scamper across Brian so as to reach the passenger window beyond which a smiling lady waits in her booth. Before I can utter a word she welcomes me by name and hands me my boarding card. I ask how she knew me, and she explained that mine was the only campervan on the ferry that night. I had considered driving all the way up through Scotland and taking the shorter ferry trip from there but this longer route seemed like it might be more fun. I do wonder though why no one else is taking their campervan on this ferry.

Soon after we are called aboard the good ship Hjaltland (the old Norse name for Shetland) and instructed to park up before firmly securing Brian's handbrake and putting him in gear, just in case it gets a bit choppy. Indeed, three different stewards have asked me to ensure the handbrake is on tight and that my gas bottle is fully shut off. They're obviously not expecting the North Sea to resemble a duck pond tonight then. I'm staying in a 4-berth (male) shared cabin with no windows. I reserve a bed with my bag (lower bunk to limit injury in the event of being tipped out by a playful sea) and go off in search of a beer. I spot Orkney Breweries' Dark Ale on tap, which goes down a treat. I've checked the menu and decided that macaroni cheese is the sensible option, rather than risk the 'vegetarian special' as these rarely live up to their billing. I settle myself down in anticipation of a fun journey ahead.

We're chugging out of port when the captain announces that he expects 35-knot winds and moderate swell. Now, 'moderate' swell has different connotations depending on what sort of swells you've experienced before. It could be anything from almost imperceptible undulations to a watery rollercoaster. The combination of the sticky tablemats, chairs chained to the floor and the captain's later correction to 'more than moderate' make me think the latter. As we exit the calmer waters, the ship starts to roll and list in a rhythmic yet unpredictable way. I tend to think of myself as being fairly immune to seasickness but I must confess that all thoughts of macaroni cheese have now left my mind, which is instead busily regretting the beer earlier. While eating would be folly, I don't feel too bad so decide to take a wander down to the bow of the ship. 'Wander' barely describes my erratic motion as I lurch around grabbing handrails and any other secure object to avoid being thrown to the ground. More worrying is the vertical motion of the ship as it creates brief weightlessness before revenging that moment of lightness with an almighty crump.

I sensibly restore myself to my former position and concentrate hard on convincing myself that I don't get seasick. I need something to focus on and the only option other than green faced passengers trying to reach the loos before their stomachs hit the eject button is the Blackpool v Huddersfield match on the telly, which the away team eventually wins 3-1, if you're interested. About 9pm I decide it might be an idea to go to bed and see the storm out from a horizontal orientation. The room is pitch black and the other three beds are already occupied - obviously my idea came a bit late. I sneak into the micro bathroom and suddenly, maybe because of the enclosed space, I am quite definitely feeling very seasick. I manage to control the twitches in my stomach as the room spins around me, dump my clothes and lie down on my bed. The nausea eases but I'm sliding around the bed involuntarily with the movements of the ship. I'm tempted to switch on the light just to see the spectacle of 4 big, hairy blokes doing synchronized bed sliding. This strange vision gently fades from my brain and the welcome torpor of sleep washes over me, broken only by the short walk for the predictable, nocturnal call of nature.

An announcement at 6:30am both wakes us up and advises us that we will dock at 8am. I fancy a shower and brekkie before driving Brian away so decide to risk disturbing the others by heading promptly for the bathroom. It's pitch dark so I try to use my iPhone for light to avoid switching on my bedside lamp. This backfires badly however when I accidentally activate the electronic voice recognition system. I can't remember its exact words but it was something akin to "switch me off and go back to bed you idiot". Shower executed I start to pack up when I hear church bells ringing. We're still far from shore so maybe it's the captain's idiosyncratic way to stir us into life. My heart sinks as I realise it's my alarm but I'm still groggy from sleep and I can't locate my phone so, regrettably, I have to switch on the light, kill the alarm, then exit promptly before any of my anonymous roommates starts complaining.

The sea is calmer now and so I venture outside to watch the sun rise as the southern tip of Shetland comes into view. This is where the main airport is situated but it's another 25 miles or so before we get to the capital, Lerwick, where we shall dock. The ripples of nausea from last night have now been replaced by waves of excitement as I stare wide-eyed at the rough-hewn beauty of our exotic destination. I check my weather app, which is showing a quite magnificent 10° Celsius, and pop back inside. I decide on tea and toast for breakfast but can't see the toast. The crew on these ships are hardened souls who no doubt suffer much worse storms than we had last night but have adapted their sense of balance to still be able to walk in a straight line carrying pints of beer or mugs of tea. Consequently I imagine they look down on the inept, rookie passenger with a degree of scorn. The following conversation won't have improved their perception of this landlubber:

"Full breakfast sir?"

"Just toast please."

"Help yourself."

"Er…where is it?"

"Right there in front of you sir."

(I see the pile of bread, look around, but can't spot the toaster)

"Er…where's the toaster please?"

"Toaster?"

"Toaster."

"It's already toasted."

"Really?"

"Really."

"All of it?"

(With a sigh) "Yes sir."

Well, that bread may once have been briefly introduced to some form of toasting apparatus but they certainly didn't engage in the kind of intimate relationship required to complete the metamorphosis from the original bread-like state. I still felt stupid though.

Brian rests after his long trip from

London to Lockerbie

3 Shetland

I experience feelings of childlike joy and bubbling anticipation as we drive slowly out of the ferry, down the ramp and off into the wilds of Shetland. We're heading for Unst, the most northerly, inhabited isle in Shetland and therefore, Britain. The scenery is bleak but quite stunning and not at all grim, with the swooping roads making for a fine drive. I soon pass my first group of Shetland ponies - lovely, colourful, pot-bellied, hairy-maned beasts. There's plenty of sheep around too and these are the most serene looking sheep I have ever seen. They seem to glow with an inner calm that I assume comes from being not just any sheep but *Shetland* sheep. My first impression of Shetland is that it's a place you could definitely love but maybe not everyone would like. It lacks the trees and mountains and streams that one may associate with typical Scottish scenery and, other than its fair share of wildlife, has few major tourist attractions. That said there's definitely a beguiling and mystical atmosphere about the place.

Unst is a two-hour drive from Lerwick, including two more short ferry crossings. As we approach the first of these I hear: "Ferry ahead! I'm warning you I might get seasick in here. I'm getting sick just thinking about it. I have to go to the bathroom. What was I saying? Oh yeah, ferry!" This would be a good time to properly introduce my satellite navigation device, Homer; so called as he has Homer Simpson's voice rather than Homer's poetic gift. I thought I'd travelled a sufficient variety of road networks by now to have heard all of his silly phrases (involving ice cream, chocolate cigars and lots of 'woo hoo's and 'doh's) but this one was new. I was already looking forward to hearing it again.

We board the first ferry and pay a very reasonable £10 to cover both crossings there and back. Yell is the loudly named island before Unst and it pretty much out-bleaks the others. I am amused however to see an advert for a social occasion that Saturday, billed as a 'Chippy Night'. This promises 'chip suppers, teas, home bakes and a raffle'. The long winter nights must fly by. We pass on the Yell nightlife opportunities, press on and soon arrive on Unst, making our way to the Baltasound hotel to park up and down a coffee. I've opted to stay the night here rather than camp, partly to mark the occasion of my first brewery but also because the only local camping option was particularly remote, dry (unthinkable) and rather Spartan. Before booking the hotel I had read that it offered 'un-serviced' rooms for only £30 a night. I don't mind roughing it a bit so I phoned up and enquired as to what exactly 'un-serviced' meant. "Basically, they're not cleaned" the helpful lady explained. "Not clean?" I exclaimed, somewhat surprised "Yes, they're clean, but they're not cleaned", she offered by way of further explanation. Wishing not to appear thick by enquiring in greater depth about a topic that seemed entirely straightforward to this lady, I began to wonder if there was a way they prevented the room getting unclean in the first place. "So, there's clean linen provided?" I asked, reaching for some specifics.

Understanding my confusion, she clarified, "the room is freshly prepared like any other, but the maid won't visit while you're staying with us". I resisted offering the response that would have surely followed if this were a Carry On movie. "So, as I'm only staying one night, the un-serviced room is no different to a serviced room?" I suggested. "Correct", she confirmed. "Right, I'll have one of those then please!"

The Valhalla Brewery, the first of the trip, is about 3 miles away from the hotel and so I decide to hire a bike to get me there. Partly for the exercise but also in the hope of a wee tasting session after the tour. Time moves slowly up here and I seem to have plenty of it to kill before my 2pm appointment. This allows me to enjoy some of the sights of Unst such as Britain's most northerly church, most northerly shop, hotel, toilet, newsagent... you name it. There's also a bus stop, originally named Bobby's bus stop after a wee lad who campaigned to stop the local Council scrapping it when it fell into disrepair, as he used it for shelter before catching the bus to school each day. These days it has become a bit of a shrine and when I visit it's bedecked in all manner of paraphernalia celebrating the Queen's 60th Jubilee. The colour scheme is a fairly lurid scarlet and the items on display include a commemorative book, a figurine of the Queen in a fetching mauve suit and, incongruously, what looks like the polar bear from Fox's Glacier Mints. The whole thing feels like a tiny, kitschy living room that happens to be particularly convenient for local transport. Obviously the buses don't come by very often up here though, as even the 'normal' bus stops offer not just the typical wee plastic bench in them but actual chairs or even an armchair! You wouldn't get away with that in London.

I stop at Foord's chocolate shop and café for lunch and I am thrilled, after last night's enforced abstinence, to see that they have macaroni cheese on the menu. This provides some useful central heating before I venture out into the cold wind and make my way to the brewery feeling more than a little excited. I'm welcomed in the doorway by Andrea, who offers to escort me around the brewery, which is housed in what used to be the RAF fire station. It's a pretty large building with room for expansion and a large space upstairs. On entering you can browse through the small shop and reception area, where they sell some local products as well as lots of beer. We're joined by a couple of locals, which takes away a degree of intimacy on my virgin tour, but offers more time for me to quietly nose around at these new and marvellous sights. This is my first brewery visit experience and it will deliver exactly what I had hoped for.

Sonny, the owner, started the brewery in 1997 after being made redundant. He'd never been in a brewery before but the council agreed to his plans and, together with a recent brewing graduate (my parents never told me you could study beer at university) they set about learning how to make beer. The brewery is named after the hall in the celestial regions, home of the Norse god Odin, where slain Viking warriors were re-borne, to be revived by a hornful of ale. A cup of tea and a biscuit just wouldn't have been very Vikingish I guess. The brewery today, while still relatively small production and quite hands-on, is rather impressive. We begin by smelling the different types of malted grains and the pungent hops. The mash tun has what looks like a 4-foot long version of the plastic stirrer you get with your cup of tea in a café resting inside it, which is patently used to mix up the grain and water. The kettle, where the sweet liquid from the mash tun is boiled with hops, is cleaned after each run, which involves someone getting inside it, scrubbing it clean then clambering out. I'm invited to have a go but I'm not sure I'd be able to get out again, assuming I ever managed to get in, so I settle for a more mundane pose for the obligatory photo. (The kettle is sometimes called a 'copper' but it actually has heating elements in the bottom so I'm sticking to 'kettle' for now.) I should advise at this point that any reader looking for in-depth technical detail is almost certainly reading the wrong book, but hang in there, it's a journey.

Next we see the fermentation vats, the cooling tanks and the bottling/labelling process. The bottling is done two at a time entirely by hand and the labels are painstakingly stuck on one at a time using a small machine. I'm interested to learn that most of the beer is filtered then bottled, rather than popped into a cask where it would continue to ferment, and is therefore not actually classed as 'real ale'. This is somewhat due to limited local demand, but also wider distribution challenges, as cask ale can only survive a few months unopened and a few days once opened. Many pubs don't know how to care properly for cask-conditioned ales and end up selling 'bad' pints to customers who then swear off ever drinking that brand again. This is my first insight into one of the recurring themes in this book - does ale have to be real to be really good? I'm looking forward to getting to the bottom of that conundrum through hours of painstaking research.

Andrea has been an excellent host, describing with vigour the history and future of the Valhalla Brewery. Among their plans is to create a bar upstairs as well as making improvements to the brewing process. They're trying to break into the Scandinavian market but with such a unique heritage you'd have to imagine countries like Japan and North America also having some appeal. I buy two bottles to take with me, the Island Bere and Simmer Dim. The former is created using a grain called 'bere' (pronounced *berr*), which is not normally used in commercial brewing and may have been introduced by 8th century Vikings. The latter's name refers to the phenomenon in mid summer when the sun only briefly dips under the horizon before reappearing minutes later. There's still time to kill before dinner so I head down to a ruined castle called Muness. Yep, you've guessed it, the most northerly castle in Britain! It's a pleasant diversion to read about the history and have a look around but I'm most impressed by the small, unlocked box cupboard, housing two excellent quality torches for the casual tourist to use during their visit then replace. You wouldn't get away with that in London.

I return to the Baltasound Hotel to enjoy a hearty dinner. I choose the locally caught haddock, cooked in Valhalla beer batter. Now, I'm actually vegetarian and only tend to have fish when no other option exists, but I can't resist marking my first brewery visit with a fresh local product made with Valhalla beer. As it happens it's delicious and after a suitable pause I decide to feast further on the sticky toffee pudding. There's a stunning sunset on the horizon, I'm nursing my third glass of merlot and suddenly doing book research seems like the best job in the world. I'm definitely learning to love Shetland and especially Unst. I read later that the Shetland Isles were given to Scotland as a dowry from the Danish Princess Margaret on the occasion of her wedding to James III in 1649. It seems like a very generous gift but I guess they still had the Faroe Islands up their sleeves. The Norse connections are strongly felt here and indeed some of the place names still have a Norse equivalent shown - we're geographically closer to Bergen than Edinburgh. Talk to the locals about the 'mainland' and they will assume you are referring to the main Shetland isle, known as, er, Mainland! Just as many Scots would support independence from the UK, so too would many Shetlanders consider independence from an independent Scotland. Ex-pats also feel a strong association with the 'Auld Rock' as it's known and I'm beginning to understand its allure.

After a long and deep sleep, my mission the next day is simply to get to Orkney by bedtime. The ferries are infrequent so I have all day to make my way back down to Lerwick before catching the evening crossing to Kirkwall. The drive back down offers a different take on the rolling, treeless scenery but Yell remains just as bleak from any direction. I have a short time to kill in Lerwick so stroll around looking for a small gift to take home. I must confess that Lerwick is not the most scenic of small towns that I have ever visited but there are a few wee shops to browse around. I pop into one and find several lines on offer that relate to Puffin poo, including a range of confectionary that doesn't entirely appeal. After some careful consideration I opt for the Puffin poo candles and I have a little chat with the young assistant. The accent here is like nothing I've heard before. It's a bit Highland as it has a certain softness and a gentle lilt, but the pronunciation is quite different. The vowels get rounded so much they almost transmute into a different letter. So, 'folk' is pronounced 'fock', 'same' is pronounced 'samm' and even 'Lerwick' is pronounced 'Larrick'. This also explains why the beer is called 'Simmer Dim' and not 'Summer Dim'. It's endearing to listen to but requires some concentration to pick it all up. As I prepare to board the ferry with Brian, I reflect on a memorable visit to a special place. They have pint-sized ponies, smiling sheep, the most northerly everything, amazing accents and puffin poo paraphernalia. I'll definitely return to Shetland one day.

There was no way I was climbing in and out of that!

4 Orkney

The ferry takes about 5 hours to cover the 120 miles to Orkney and the sea is mercifully much calmer than for the crossing from Aberdeen to Lerwick, which apparently enjoys legendary status for the awful conditions and consequent scenes of people and furniture sliding around in half-digested food. I'm feeling confident enough about my internal food management system this evening to tuck into the vegetable curry before buying a ticket for the on-board cinema, which tonight is showing Prometheus. Being stuck in a windowless room in the middle of a mildly undulating ship seems to add a bit of atmosphere to the Alien prequel and soon we're approaching Kirkwall harbour.

I get to the Kirkwall Youth Hostel just before it closes for the night. Frank, a Dutch/American guy who writes fiction in the winter months and earns the cash to support his craft in the summer, checks me in and furnishes me with a copy of his latest book. My room however hasn't been furnished with very much at all and is entirely Spartan but functional. It's also cheap so I have no complaints at all. I learn that the building I'm in was once an army barracks, which makes complete sense, as the room has nothing other than the minimum required for sleeping. I'd already read about the complete lack of power sockets so got all charged up on the way over. However, I imagine this place probably slept about four squaddies to a room, so I'm grateful for the relative luxury. I'm alone in a simple, cold cell, miles from home and every noise that breaks the eerie silence sets my imagination into overdrive. So far I've slept in a van, on a ferry, in an un-serviced room and now in solitary confinement. I also haven't had a (proper) drink today so sleep is slow to arrive. (Reading that sentence again I cringe at the conclusions that one may draw about my drinking habits. Whilst alcohol is usually sufficient to precipitate sleep, I can confirm that it is not always necessary!) I wake to the grim view of more barracks outside but the sun is threatening to appear so I shower and go find breakfast in downtown Kirkwall. The options on offer don't get anywhere close to the 'big and healthy' New York style or even the traditional London 'greasy spoon' but needs must. Eventually I find somewhere that offers some promise but delivers little more than hot fluids and edible calories.

Before leaving town I feel duty bound to visit the Highland Park distillery, where they create one of the most famous and well-liked whiskies in the world. I squeeze Brian into the car park only to discover that reception doesn't open until ten o'clock and that's a tad late for a man with work to do, so I head off for another day at the office. Orkney has two breweries, conveniently located quite close to each other. On paper (or online to be more exact) they seem quite disparate in style if not location and indeed this proves to be the case.

The Swannay Brewery is run by Rob Hill, a very engaging chap for whom brewing seems to be a labour of love - a lot of labour, but also a lot of love. When I meet him I'm not expecting much more than a handshake as his assistant has gone home ill and there's clearly plenty to do. But this man's capacity for work is matched only by his enthusiasm and before I know it I'm trotting around after him as he simultaneously attends to admin matters, brews beer, gives me a very informative tour, describes all his future plans and delivers grain in a fork-lift. I'm taking a liking to hop smelling and I notice a similarity in scent to cannabis, which I share with Rob (my observation, not my cannabis). He confirms that the two plants are related and indeed there's no reason why hemp couldn't be used to flavour a beer. Using actual cannabis or skunk however, incorporating the active ingredient THC, might be frowned upon by HM Customs & Excise, not to mention the local constabulary, various religious groups, my mum and most traditional drinkers.

As Rob's on his own he's brewing today in the original equipment that he set up many years ago. While these containers look like they've been in a demolition derby they seem to function just as well as the shiny new production line sitting proudly adjacent to them. The wort flows from the mash tun into an underback, which allows Rob to inspect the colour, smell, taste and viscosity of the sweet liquid before it makes its way to the kettle. He seems finely tuned to the needs of every valve and lever and dashes around tweaking several to achieve the desired effect on the final product. The building that holds all of this alcoholic alchemy is given further character by a giant Union flag hanging at one end. He kindly presents me with a small bottle of 9% porter which I keep to warm me up one cold evening in Brian. The brewery is made up of several old farm buildings once used to make an apparently excellent cheese. If Rob's dreams come to fruition, he'll have a visitor centre, bar, restaurant and accommodation as well as increased brewing capacity. I get the feeling that he loves the journey, the struggle and the hard-earned successes and maybe would be a little bored if ever everything ran like clockwork and his dream suddenly became reality.

Just down the road is the Orkney Brewery, resplendent in its purpose-built visitor centre, all shiny and new and created to a high specification. The style is not untypical of visitor centres up and down the country and the scale of investment tells a story about the brewery, which is owned by a hotelier. Orkney insist that based on global sales they are the largest independent brewery in Scotland, but BrewDog (we'll come to them later) and perhaps others may contest this claim. Certainly, they send bottles all over the world and during my visit there's a big tanker into which vats of beer are being pumped to be taken away for bottling. They do cask-conditioned ales here also but these are sold only in the UK.

I'm given a pleasant tour and invited to smell and taste the various barley malts that are used to create the wide variety of beers. I am assured by my host that toasted barley is also used to make the Camp coffee mixture that I recall my father having on the table when I was a young lad. Later research however reveals that Camp coffee was made mostly from chicory while roasted barley was actually the main ingredient in Nestle Caro. I haven't ever heard of this product before but I'm interested to note that a cheap coffee substitute has a name that translates as 'expensive' in Spanish! I'm also intrigued to learn that hop pellets rather than hop flowers are being used in the brewing process here. They insist that the flavours are unaffected but CAMRA (Campaign for Real Ale) needed persuading that the product could still be classed as real ale. The pellets remind me (in look, not smell) of the food they throw to farmed fish, invoking a wild feeding frenzy; not an image I had expected a brewery to conjure up. As our journey progresses we shall hear arguments for and against pellets but my instinct is to wonder why you wouldn't use the actual flowers. Meantime, there's a bloke in fetching yellow wellies emptying the large mash tun of the spent barley grains. These do not go to waste however as they are used for local cattle feed. They smell all right actually (the grains, not the cattle) and no doubt there's still plenty nutrition in them for the bovine diners.

There's a tasting at the end and my host kindly extends the offer of all five draught beers on tap that day instead of the usual three. I've still got some driving to do so I just neck half of each 1/3 pint tasting glass. Well, except for the Golden Amber, which is my favourite and is therefore fully necked. I calculate that 4 halves and a whole from five 1/3 pint glasses sums neatly to a pint overall. I'm just under the limit but decide to stay for lunch just in case. As I enjoy my relaxed repast, I'm directly facing the bar at the end of the restaurant, which is entirely stocked with colourful bottles of the range of beers made here. I can't fault the whole set-up as a well run, if typical, visitor centre experience, not unlike those that you may experience at most distilleries. One can certainly contrast and compare with the more, er, organic approach at Swannay up the road, but do these differences tell us anything about the quality of the final product? What are the secrets to making a perfect pint? This is another question for us to explore, dear reader, as we continue our journey.

Next stop is Stromness where we shall board the ferry for Scrabster on the British mainland, a short drive from Thurso where we'll camp for the night. Stromness is the venue for the Orkney Folk Festival held each May and by all accounts it's one wild party from start to finish. A cornucopia of crammed bars, more musicians than you could shake a bow at, a stunning array of facial hair and a riot of chunky knit sweaters. I can't stand listening to fiddly fiddle music for anything more than five minutes at a time but by all accounts this festival is something to be experienced at least once in a lifetime. I've only had a brief taste of Orkney on my first visit, so I'm very tempted to return one year, whether just to enjoy the permanent attractions or perhaps to indulge in a few days of ale-fuelled concerts and ceilidhs. I would also be intrigued to see how Rob's plans have come to fruition a few years hence.

As I board the ferry I reflect on how different the two sets of islands are. Shetland really felt like another planet. It is indeed quite otherworldly with its absence of trees, ancient Norse roots and significant distance from mainland Britain. And that accent! Orkney seems the more prosperous and tourist-friendly of the two and perhaps offers a wider range of attractions, without one having to experience the dreaded ferry trip to Lerwick. It's also probably a softer landing for your first northerly isles experience, but if you like it rugged and bleak, distant and intriguing then you might find something special in Shetland. Indeed, I might just time my return for the Simmer Dim.

The ferry docks and Brian and I make the short trip to the campsite on the edge of Thurso. It's run by an American gentleman who checks me out and checks me in before giving me directions to a decent bar not far away. He tells me that they often hold ceilidhs for the locals so, ever ready to engage with a Dashing White Sergeant, I head up after scoffing my tasty risotto. Well, there's barely room in there to Strip a Willow and no signs of life other than tables full of local blokes arguing loudly about various manly pursuits. I settle down at the bar for a pint, free Wi-Fi and some footie on the telly before retiring for the night in Brian on the peaceful shores of Thurso. As I drift off into sleep I muse that lying in the back of a van, with the curtains closed, does feel a little like resting in the back of a hearse. Sorry Brian.

The drive to Inverness airport the next morning for my weekend flight home is quite stunning with fabulous views out to sea and across the hills. The rainbows perfectly present all their colours and sit so high in the sky that they almost seem to touch ends at the bottom. I break my journey with a brief visit to the Glenmorangie distillery, as much to use their facilities as anything else. I've just missed a tour and can't find any toilets so carry on to Tain from whence came the men entrusted with the secrets of the nectar produced up the road. Refreshed, we arrive at Inverness airport and I manage to park Brian in the wrong car park, pull all his curtains so that he can have a private kip pending my return and then realise my mistake. I drive him to the space I actually booked with his curtains still closed, which makes some of the manoeuvres very tricky indeed. As I make my way through security they suspiciously examine my puffin poo candle. Their concern is less whether it may be made from some explosive substance instead of wax, and more that it's slightly too large at 110ml. With a shrug of the Security's shoulders I get to keep my candle despite the potential terrorist risks. You wouldn't get away with that in London!

These are hops and should not

be confused with cannabis

5 Water

"Beer is proof that God loves us and wants us to be happy."

Benjamin Franklin

"The water's for cleaning and the liquor's for the beer." This was one of the early lessons I learned about beer on my travels. I can't remember who said it first but I heard it quite a few times. So maybe I should have called this chapter 'Liquor' but that would have been confusing. When the brewers refer to liquor they are indeed talking about water, probably much the same water that is used for cleaning everything out. The differentiation comes not from what it is but what it's intended to be used for. This means that the storage tanks used for water intended for brewing are called hot and cold liquor tanks. Not every brewery uses or needs a cold liquor tank, depending on their water supply and scale, and some smaller breweries will double up their hot liquor tank as the kettle. So, liquor is definitely the correct term but for ease of reference I'm going to call it water from here on anyway. Mostly.

Before proceeding, I should explain why we have, er, parked Brian for a chapter to talk about water. The main purpose of this journey was to discover beer in the land of whisky. I started that journey with nothing but the most basic knowledge of what went into beer and how it was made. I'd picked up previously that many quality European beers used only four ingredients – water, barley, hops and yeast. This, I was to learn, is just the tip of the iceberg, the head on the pint if you will. There is so much more to the art and science of brewing beer and so it seemed like a good idea to pause our journey occasionally to delve into the brewer's world. It also seemed like a good idea to tackle one key ingredient at a time then chuck everything else into a 'beer' chapter. So, I do hope you enjoy our occasional deviations but if you're bored by the thought of these 'educational' chapters, do feel free to leaf forward and re-join the journey in chapter six. Or maybe you could return here after the journey is complete and tackle these five tangential chapters together in one go? I should though, at this point, offer the technically minded readers a warning, and the low boredom threshold folk (if you're still with us) some comfort. I am thoroughly under-qualified to get too deeply into any of this and will probably over-simplify (or completely misrepresent) anything remotely complex. This is something of a beginner's guide, written by an absolute beginner, which will furnish you with enough information and insight to feel comfortable talking with beer people, without providing the ammunition to empty a bar with your bottomless beer banter. Still here? Cool, let's talk about water then.

You may have occasionally seen people wearing t-shirts with the slightly funny, vaguely annoying proclamation, 'drink beer, save water'. Had t-shirt slogans been around in mediaeval times then they may have said 'drink beer, avoid water' as it was much safer to quench one's thirst with the mildly alcoholic ales (that had been through a boiling process) than risk drinking the foul, disease-ridden water. At least that was the excuse offered at the time. While drinking beer to save water appears to be a solid rationale on the surface, it is of course far from true. In the brewing process typically 5 litres of water are used for every litre of beer produced. Having watched the brewing process many times I have to assume that most of the extra 4 litres are for cleaning as very little of the initial liquor doesn't end up in the beer. Water preservation buffs will point out that in fact up to 180 litres can be needed for every litre of beer if you account for all the irrigation and goodness knows what else needed to create the key ingredients. I think that's going a bit too far, especially when you consider how much more water is needed to create, say, the oranges used in orange juice. I don't think beer is any less water efficient than most beverages and I recommend that you continue to drink it without unduly troubling your conscience.

So, let's for now just concentrate on the 'liquor' that goes into the actual brewing process and stays in the beer. You might think (as I did) that water is the least important and influential of the main ingredients in beer. It would be folly to dismiss it so easily though, as it does of course constitute the vast majority of the final product that you so enjoy – up to 97% in fact. That's probably not a great surprise but let's consider for a moment the world of beer advertising. They may talk about hops or barley, if they mention ingredients at all, but how often do you hear someone say, "Ooh, you can taste the quality of the water in that beer!". You may laugh at the very thought of praising the water in an alcoholic drink but that's exactly what the whisky buffs will do if you give them half a chance. Question more deeply though and the truth emerges that the water has very limited impact on the flavour of whisky. There will be some minor effect depending on how mineral rich (hard) the water is and whether it has run through peaty ground or not, but we're talking details. My suspicion is that water affects the flavour and quality of beer just as much and probably more, than whisky. This makes sense (to me at least) as beer retains its water through to the end product whereas whisky is made by distilling the alcohol from the water, which is then essentially left behind. I may have ambled quite far along the plank of controversy in making that last statement but hopefully I didn't fall off the end.

Many brewers jokingly say that making beer is 95% easy (because that's the water part), it's just the other 5% that's difficult. So, does water just make the beer wet or does it influence what you taste from your glass? Burton on Trent is a town and major brewing area in Staffordshire, England. The water there has high gypsum content and lends itself particularly well to creating hoppy pale ales for which the area is famous. So famous indeed that, brewers making similar beers in different areas where the water is softer, will add gypsum to 'Burtonise' the water. Gypsum is also known as calcium sulphate dihydrate and you may have first come across it in its processed (after heating to 150°C) form, which we would all refer to as Plaster of Paris. There are other examples of how a particular type of water works best in making a specific type of beer. In Ireland for instance the water is hard as it contains a lot of calcium carbonate (chalk) and this is ideal for creating stout (funnily enough). In the Czech Republic, the water is very soft and works very well in the creation of light lagers such as Pilsner. It's all starting to make sense isn't it? There is of course no reason why you can't make any style of beer you like using whatever water presents itself at your brewery, but there's also no doubt that some waters work better than others.

I always ask the brewer where he gets his water and how, if at all, he treats it. (None have yet answered "like one of the family"). Some just shrug and say "straight from the tap". Further probing may reveal that this first passes through a purifier while others may have a water treatment system handy to prepare the 'liquor' for the beer. Many places I visited enjoyed deliciously soft water, offering a blank canvas to start from so you can then add exactly the salts you require for the particular beer you're making that day. Getting that right also adds to the mash efficiency by helping to maximise the sugars that are extracted. A few breweries are lucky enough to have a local spring that brings some unique character to the beer, at least in the marketing blurb. Scotland's water is generally soft, sometimes incredibly soft. Living in London you probably go through twice as much soap and detergents as someone in Inverness as it's that much harder to create a lather with hard water. The Scots get in a lather no problem at all.

Cleaning takes up a great deal of the brewer's time and he will very happily delegate this task to an assistant or, if he can afford it, install an automatic system. The floor gets pretty messy so you need wellies, a hose and a sloping floor with a drain. The mash tun needs carefully cleaned once the spent grains have been dispatched and exactly the same is true of the kettle. One of the messiest phases of the brew though happens in the fermentation vats (FVs), due to the activity of the yeast. Brewers will generally avoid filling these too full as otherwise the sticky, frothy mess spills over and encrusts itself on to the outside of the tanks as well as the mess that it leaves on the inside. Cleaning the FVs is even more important than the mash tun or kettle as at this stage there will be no further boiling to kill off any nasty things that remain. So someone has to get inside these vessels and give them a right good scrub! This requires lots of water and typically caustic soda (sodium hydroxide) for cleaning purposes and peracetic acid for sterilising purposes. Doing this properly and thoroughly is absolutely critical to avoid the next batch of beer being ruined or, worse, poisoning your customers. So, for every day you brew, you also have to clean out the whole system before being able to start again the next day. Keep a clean brewery, brew tasty beers - I definitely found a correlation between the two.

So, a small-scale brewer has to have, or acquire, quite a range of skills. Before we even get on to the business and marketing side of things, he has to be a bit of a chemist, a decent chef and a pernickety cleaner. If you wanted to get all scientific about it you could analyse your water, agonise over the salt and mineral content and keep detailed notes of exactly how each variation affects the final product. Many brewers come with a background in chemistry, some learn about the details at university and some just come with loads of experience and trust their nose and tongue without overdoing the scientific equations. At the end of the day the customer will either like or love the pint they're drinking, probably without thinking too much about the part that water, or liquor, played in its creation. Little do they know…

6 Cromarty to Stornoway

EasyJet delivers me on time to Inverness airport and the transfer to the offsite parking awaits my arrival. Brian starts at the second attempt and belches a large plume of smoke from his exhaust. Pardon him. I make a note to always check that there aren't any humans or animals within a ten-metre radius when I start him up after a few days idle. Having topped up with some cheap Tesco diesel we head across the Moray Firth, up and through Cromarty to the brewery bearing the name of this pretty corner of Scotland. I'm a tad peckish so stop at a small village on the way for a snack and take the opportunity to indulge in a macaroni cheese pie. Growing up in Dundee I didn't have the best of diets. One of the worst examples was deep fried pizza. These were virtually ubiquitous and it never even dawned on me that they might not be the best choice for nutrition and health. They weren't even good pizzas that were then deep fried but, au contraire, appeared custom made for the purpose, eschewing tasty toppings for plenty dough that could easily soak up lots of oil. I must confess though that one or two gourmet chippies did make an effort to create something that was relatively fresh and tasty, but this was rare. At least I never had the deep fried mince pie, a great favourite in Glasgow, known lovingly as the heartstopper! I can also confirm that I have resisted the deep fried Mars Bar thus far in my life. Anyway, the reason for this divergence is that macaroni cheese pies are one delicacy from my youth that still cause involuntary salivation, hence sparking my indulgence. This one, happily, is a fine example of the breed, managing to be moist inside with a crusty top and light pastry. It's almost delicatessen standard and you can actually taste the cheese. Tummy filled, I can proceed to my first brewery of the week.

I'm looking forward to this one more than most, not just because I like the feel of it from the website or that Jenni has been very welcoming to this strange bloke wanting to visit their family brewery, but also because they are distant kin, sharing my paternal ancestral surname. I'm sure this does no harm in ensuring the warm welcome I receive on arrival. Indeed, I have a nice cup of tea and a biscuit in my hands in no time at all. Jenni introduces me to son Craig who is the brew master of the family having ditched a sensible engineering degree to secure a brewing qualification at Heriot-Watt. (Again, why didn't someone point me in that direction when I was 18?) The brewery is spanking new having been constructed just last year with brewing having started less than a year ago. Progress has been swift with their first award standing proudly on the reception desk when I arrive. Emblazoned across the front of the desk is their slogan 'beer worth believing in'. The brewery is large and modern with obvious room for expansion and, out here in this stunning countryside, seems like a pretty good place to work.

Before long Craig's taking me around the hi-tech equipment sourced from Hungary and we're joined by mum, dad and Bailey the dog. They don't filter or pasteurise any beers here (actually, Bailey takes no part in the brewing process whatsoever), whether they're destined for the cask, keg or bottle. They do use finings though, which is standard practice in order to create the clarity in the beer that customers expect. Un-fined beers need a particularly refined drinker to enjoy the extra taste and not be troubled by the cloudy pint.

The hops used here come from New Zealand, USA and Slovenia. The yeast is a special strain developed at source and there are myriad types of barley in the storeroom. I'm treated to a tasting of three of the beers, direct from the conditioning tanks, including a rather cheeky 6.7% IPA that is yet to be named or launched. I comment that it's stronger than most IPAs you see in bars but Craig counters that this one would therefore actually make it all the way to India, no problem at all. India Pale Ales originally got that name as they were made for export to the thirsty folk living out in the sub-continent colony and had to be more alcoholic and hoppy to survive the journey. Any excuse. It's the Middleton family lunchtime now so I head off with three bottles from the range, a bottle opener and a badge saying 'I'm a Happy Chappy', that being the name of their first ever brew and the one recently honoured by CAMRA.

It's a short drive to the Black Isle Brewery. The Black Isle is not actually an island but a peninsula and is called Black because it's not white. Apparently snow doesn't lie here for some reason so it stands out from the neighbouring areas in the winter months. The brewery is at the end of a bumpy wee road and the premises here are also pretty new, although the brewery's been around for nearly ten years, recently moving in to its new home. The visitor centre gives the impression of a successful business and the tour is both free and delivered with a panache that suggests its been given more than a few times. The 'usp' here is that the beer is entirely organic, the only such brewery in Scotland. They even have a local malter with organic credentials. The barley is grown next door and the water comes from a local borehole. They also have a natty new bottling machine that can get through 2,000 bottles an hour so demand must be high.

I learn that each September they hold a beer and music festival called Jocktober where about 1,000 people come to camp, chill, drink and dance. 'The greatest Scottish beer festival in the world' is their proud claim and it definitely sounds like one for the diary. Having expanded at home, they've also broken into the Japanese market and are looking to export to the USA next. There's a tasting of four beers at the end, which I'm pleased to see (as a driver) is offered in micro-cups. They're exactly the shape of a typical pint glass but only 4cm tall. I amuse myself for a few minutes trying out some photos that make it look like a giant's hand is holding a pint before noticing that the host has stopped speaking and the other punters are giving me funny looks.

I dutifully buy a couple of bottles including one made with oats as well as barley. I refer to it as porridge stout but that doesn't seem to meet with approval. I do now have a decent cellarful of beer so I resolve to diminish my stocks this week to ease Brian's load and stop him listing to one side. It's been a very pleasant day and it's time to head down toward Beauly where I nab a late lunch before camping up by the banks of the river where several fishermen are trying their luck just upstream of the bridge. I'm aware that I'm playing Russian roulette with my gas supplies when I need them nightly to cook and stay warm but I still haven't figured out the solution. Supplies at least see me through this cold evening and the Happy Chappy nicely washes down my rather tasty pepper and goat's cheese frittata. To help stave off the cold I decide to next try the Hibernator Oatmeal stout before sleep engulfs me.

The drive to Gairloch the next morning presents an ever-changing picture of rugged wilderness, viewed through first rain then sun to create rainbows so large that I can see exactly where the pot of gold would be. I'm almost tempted to go take a look, just in case. No time for that however as we have two brewery appointments before getting to Ullapool for the evening ferry to Lewis. The Old Inn enjoys a rather splendid setting in Gairloch, which itself has been blessed with terrific views out across the Atlantic Ocean. The brewery here is very much of the micro variety, the smallest I have yet seen, set up purely to serve the needs of the hotel and residing in a shed, with a capacity of some 100 litres - the brewery that is, not the shed. It pretty much looks the same as the kit I've seen elsewhere but shrunk down to fit in this tiny, enclosed space. It's originally from the USA so there are quirky names like the 'Therminator' for the heat exchanger. They have four beers here that are made one at a time and rotated in the bar along with an occasional special creation. Indeed, I'm told that the hotel hosted the Beekeepers Association last weekend and they went to the trouble of creating a honey ale just for them called The Bees Knees. Apparently there was a real buzz about the place…

I have a chat to Mike, creator of these splendid beers, about brewing and brewers and explain that I am next off to An Teallach where I am aware, from an earlier phone call, that visitors are not normally received. Mike then regales me with a story of one poor chap (American I think) who dropped in unannounced to ask to see the brewery only to be told to f*ck off. I wish he hadn't told me that. I'm pretty hungry now (and in no hurry to tackle An Teallach) so I decide to have lunch at the hotel, selecting from the 'healthy' section. My mushroom, lentil and leek pie, chips and peas are excellent but also a serious size of portion. I check back at the menu to find what it actually said was 'for the healthier appetite', which is not the same thing at all!

It's a cracking coastal drive from Gairloch and I soon arrive at the village of Camusnagaol to look for the An Teallach Brewery. (An Teallach is the name of the local mountain and means 'forge' or 'anvil' in Gaelic.) This is a tiny village on the shores of Little Loch Broom (Loch Brush would have been more original) but I drive through three times without spotting any signs or indications of the brewery. Luckily it's up for sale and so there's a photo of the house online on an agent's website. I make my fourth pass of the village and there it is. Bingo. It seems like no one's at home but I really want to see every brewery in Scotland so I sheepishly creep in and indeed, creep up, on poor Wilma who's just finished a brew. She remembers my call and so I'm allowed to stay and we have a bit of chat about the brewery (and campervans – Brian's a great icebreaker) and I enquire about how the sale's going. Apparently most interested buyers come with little or no brewing experience but plenty of romantic notions. The advert explains that turnover is £162,000 with net profits of £63,000. This is a 9-barrel plant, which means that each production run can yield 36 casks (or firkins), which translates to over 2,500 pints. I'm a little tempted by the sale myself given the beautiful setting, nice house and successful brewery on offer for less than my place in London is worth. I'd miss the easy access to gigs though.

With two more bottles of beer kindly donated by Wilma safely stowed in Brian I head around (Big) Loch Broom to Ullapool and park him up for the night in a free car park next to Tesco. He appears somewhat relieved not be suffering another ferry journey, his services not being required, as the brewery in Stornoway is a stone's throw from the harbour. Being a foot passenger also means that the ticket is a mere £16.40 return. The ferry hums its way out of port toward its Hebridean destination and the hills stretch either side of us like a guard of honour from the mountain regiment. I keep a look out for dolphins or porpoises but they're keeping their heads down and soon the sun has set and I'm looking out at two shades of grey that meet at the distant horizon. The three-hour journey passes quickly and as we near Stornoway a Coastguard helicopter hangs just above our stern to see us safely into port. Sweet.

After we dock I walk to the Heb hostel where I'll be kipping for the night. I'd been warned that they had a party of 21 staying but they had still managed to find me a bed. I'd seen a large group of young people on the ferry who were being shepherded around by a small bloke in a kilt - Awesome Haggis tours or some such. Right enough they all pile into the Heb so I grab a top bunk at the back of the dorm and sneak out in search of a pub where I can watch the footie. As I stroll around I'm decidedly un-tempted by the array of dimly lit traditional boozers containing a few scattered punters apparently immune to the smell coming from the beer-stained carpets. I'm outside looking in but nonetheless remain confident of that nasal assessment. I settle instead for a smart hotel bar where there's no footie but no smell either and for a change to my liquid diet I enjoy a couple of glasses of wine. I retire early, resisting the temptation to join the happy Haggis throng downstairs.

The next day I set off in search of the Hebridean Brewery, feeling a little tired having been woken up on several occasions by my snoring companions. One person snoring is fine I find, as you can tune out to the rhythm. With several, however, the beat is unpredictable and therefore disturbing. Inexplicably, after an evening without beer, my bladder also wakes me twice. Maybe I should lay off the water. There's a free breakfast at the hostel but the kitchen is tiny, provisions limited and hungry punters abound. I therefore repair to the hotel next door for some decent scran, peace and quiet, all served up for £6.50. After brekkie I head to the brewery only to find it completely deserted. I try ringing their number and, while the ringing sound from within confirms I'm in the right place, there's no answer. I can see the funny side of coming all the way to Lewis to visit a brewery that's closed but

I'm still disappointed. I retreat to the hostel with my tail between my legs and lazily browse the local newspaper, which heralds the news that Lewis has the third most expensive fuel after Norway and Turkey. Who'd have thought? The hostel noticeboard offers little more of interest and under the jaunty 'what's happening' section someone has written 'not much'.

There's only an hour until the ferry and no response to the message I left but I optimistically decide to swing by on my way to port. To my delight and relief there are signs of life and in no time John is welcoming me in for a short tour. The brewery is in a fairly large building and uses what you may describe as old school kit. Valves and levers take precedence over buttons and screens. I compare it to Jack White eschewing digital technology to record in old analogue studios. The brewery, led by Andy, seems to embrace the hands-on approach even at the cost of higher production levels. I can't help thinking that with some investment the business here could really grow as they have a strong angle being the only Outer Hebridean brewery. Their website however seems very out of date as the latest news item was from January 2005 and begins jauntily with: "Too cold, too dark, too wet, too windy, too hung over, too broke & nobody wants beer".

This brewery does however seem close to the community and John explains that new recipes are developed before being tested out on some lucky punters. Indeed, the Post Office across the road provides a ready supply of eager volunteers for tasting sessions held as they knock off work. They only bottle four beers from their range and John kindly furnishes me with one of each as I depart, including the Berserker, naked without its label, which at 7.5% just breaches the Government's higher duty levels, making it too expensive to market. I wish them well in their battle to convince HM Custom & Excise that 7.45% would be a more accurate estimate of its ABV (Alcohol By Volume).

I return to Ullapool and drive Brian back across Scotland to Dingwall where we spend the night at a campsite right next to Ross County's football ground. I'm checked in by a very unpleasant woman who berates me for not having my membership card to hand, before following an old bloke on a bike (me not her) to my allocated pitch. The weather's being kind, there are wee bunnies everywhere and I have a wide choice of excellent beers with which to accompany my dinner. The pick of these is the 9% porter from Rob at the Swannay Brewery, which is quite delicious. I make a brief visit to the welcoming local bar but I'm disappointed to see that it doesn't offer any real ales. All too often the household name beers abound and leave no space for the local craft products, which is rather a shame. Nonetheless I stay for a pint and reflect on the last few days. I've seen five breweries, each with quite a different story to tell, enjoyed some splendid scenery, briefly visited the lovely island of Lewis and survived An Teallach. I think the macaroni cheese pie was the highlight though.

There was a real buzz about

the place that weekend

7 Loch Ness to Loch Leven

Loch Ness is probably known across the developed world, not least because of its frequent suffix, 'Monster'. Whomever came up with the legend of Nessie, perhaps unwittingly, gave the local tourism business a huge shot in the arm that continues today, even though science has finally put to bed the possibility of her existence. However, Loch Ness merits all of this attention even without its famous tenant. It is the largest loch in Scotland by volume and indeed there is more fresh water in there than all the lakes of England and Wales combined. It's very deep at 230m but not our deepest. That honour goes to Loch Morar, home of another fabled monster called Morag - surely an attempt to jump on the monster bandwagon.

Given the recognition that Loch Ness can attach to anything bearing its name, it's a wonder that it hasn't been protected by copyright. It hasn't and therefore we can today visit the Loch Ness Brewery, in the grounds of the Benleva hotel in the wonderfully named village of Drumnadrochit. Their strapline claims that 'now there's something new in the water'. I meet with Allan, former fisheries biologist, and George who've been running the brewery for about 5 years together with Allan's brother Steve. They explain that the brewery provides casks to the hotel and two other hostelries nearby, keeping their wee production line pretty busy. They are however about to open a new facility to enable some expansion and might even get into bottling their ales one day. We have a good natter about other breweries, some of which I can now talk about from first hand knowledge, which gives me that wee warm glow of the recently initiated. They also explain that they hold two festivals a year, the main one being in late summer, where beer and music are the centre of attention. I make a note to start populating my 2013 diary with some of these shindigs, perhaps as an alternative book promotion tour!

I also bonded with Allan over our love of campervans, having spotted his VW Transporter parked near Brian. We compared our experiences and I recognise all too clearly Allan's description of struggling up hills with just a 1.6 litre diesel engine pushing a fairly heavy vehicle. As you know, I had suffered this same fate many times, only keeping forward momentum by engaging second or even first gear, but causing poor Brian to overheat and request a rest stop. I share this story with Allan who empathises with every word but is stuck for a cure. I take him through my broken turbo story and explain the consequent boost in performance. He's grateful for the tip and resolves to get his mechanic mate to check it out post haste in return for a few pints. I'm sure Allan's 'Brian' will be feeling like a new van after the surgery and will soon be racing up the hilly highland highways.

A splendid drive around the top of the loch and down the Spey Valley takes me past the 'Osprey village' of Boat of Garten and on to Aviemore, Scotland's leading ski resort. In the days before European ski locations came within reach of most punters, this was the place to come. It probably snowed more then too so the skiing would have been more reliable. Scotland still offers some great skiing when the conditions are right but you just can't predict when that's going to happen or how long it's going to last. Aviemore grew to accommodate this demand for its sport and scenery but of course that all changed with the advent of milder winters, cheaper flights abroad and higher disposable incomes and it was allowed to become a bit of a ghost resort. Happily it's found its feet again in a way that attracts year-round visitors to enjoy the stupendous wildlife and glorious surrounding countryside, but Chamonix it ain't.

The Cairngorm Brewery is of the 'set up for visitors' variety with a free tour and generous tasting to follow. Our guide spends about a quarter of our allocated time taking us on a short but insightful tour before getting down to the important bit where we taste what seems like about ten beers. Anyone in the shop not on the tour is also invited to join in and I'm sure any passers by would have been hauled in as well for good measure. So we squash up in the wee tasting room, working our way through the range from light to dark. Our host has arranged us in an arc by the wall, facing the crescent shaped bar that curves across the room. The beers are served in strict left to right rotation, returning to start again with a new brew like a high-speed poker dealer, dishing out ales instead of aces. I'm taking it slowly with Brian's wellbeing in mind but others are taking full advantage of our host's generosity. I can now understand why they distributed us next to the wall, as additional support will, for some, soon be required. As we imbibe our way through their range, we learn that Cairngorm Gold and Sheepshaggers Gold are in fact the same beer but given different names depending on whether they are destined for posh folk in Peterborough or punters in Peterhead. Some of the beers have unusual flavourings such as blueberries or milk thistle and ginger. I'm not a fan of mucking about with something as perfect in its simplicity as beer but I guess it has its attractions to some.

I note that the Vegetarian Society has approved the beers, which surprises me as we learned that these are fined with isinglass, made from the swim bladders of sturgeon. (Quite how someone made that connection is beyond me. Were they perhaps using the inedible organ as a makeshift container for beer when someone noticed the cloudy substance had miraculously cleared?) I'm informed however that only the cask ales are fined as the stuff in the bottles has been filtered which obviates the need for being bladdered - maybe that's where that expression came from?

I buy a bottle of the Black Gold, the darkest one of the range, and make my way south to Pitlochry where we will camp for the night. It's an absolutely beautiful day and therefore a spectacular drive around the edge of the Cairngorms National Park. The campsite is just over the river from the town centre, near the Festival Theatre where Arsenic and Old Lace is running alongside its repertory chums. The campsite has free Wi-Fi and fabulous ablution facilities, where you essentially choose any one of several fully integrated units with toilet/shower/sink provided. Once Brian is settled in I stroll over the Dam and Fish Ladder (sounds like another great curse to me) into town where I neck a pint of Ossian before treating myself to a very decent Vegetable Dhansak Balti in the local Indian.

It's a clear sky, which is a clear sign that it's going to freeze tonight. I get Brian as warm as I can with his wee heater but in no time my head starts to chill and I have to duck under the duvet, before coming out again for air. Brian operates something like a coolbox in these circumstances. Once you get him cold, he stays cold. I might even manufacture some campervan shaped coolboxes one day. How cool would those be? After an unpleasantly cold night I resolve to get my sleeping bag into action henceforth. There's a frost across the grass, the temperature has probably just broken into the positive integers and it looks like another stunning day ahead.

My first stop is at the Moulin Inn up the back of town where I'm expecting to meet the brewer for a tour of the microbrewery that serves the hotel. I arrive, only to be informed, rather too cheerily, by the receptionist that Mike (the brewer) has gone off on two weeks holiday. Clearly a snap decision as I had only made the appointment last week. I'm disappointed but there's nothing I can do and at least Pitlochry is an easy place to re-visit given its fairly central position in Scotland. There is also a sliver of silver lining as I can now catch up on some long overdue chores. So, Brian gets his oil and anti-freeze topped up and a hot, soapy wash to boot. I also finally procure myself a replacement gas bottle and UK regulator to replace the Dutch kit when its gas finally expires (any day soon).

Blessed with spare time, I decide to head for Aberfeldy to try and find one of the newest breweries in Scotland, Strathbraan. Finding any information on this brewery has proved challenging and it's only after I've parked up in Aberfeldy that I check my notes to find that actually it's in Dunkeld. Doh - can't blame Homer for that one. I haven't been able to find any contact details either so I'll be dropping in unannounced. Using postcodes to track down an address in remote places is a fairly futile exercise I have learned. This once again proves to be the case, as I take a very sharp left down a muddy drive before realising I am invading someone's private residence. Before some red-faced farmer starts marching toward me with his 12-bore shotgun I frantically swing Brian back onto the road and accelerate away. When I finally find my prey, I park next to the 'No Parking, Private Property' sign and go see if there's anyone home. It's a lovely big property with an intercom at the gate, but I get no response and can't see any signs of life. The brewery building is clear to see so I take a few snaps, reluctantly retrieve Brian and consider Plan C. This really isn't turning out to be the most productive brewery day of the trip so far.

In order to salvage at least one successful visit I call Inveralmond Brewery whose Ossian beer I had enjoyed the previous evening and they kindly invite me to come right along for an impromptu tour with Ken, the boss. I immediately make my way to the brewery, which is on an industrial estate on the outskirts of Perth and presents rather an impressive set-up. It's scale comfortably puts it in the top ten I would say and it also appears fairly high-tech. Nonetheless, Ken's expert ears and eyes are never off duty while he explains the history and challenges of the brewery and he often darts off to make an adjustment or close a valve. So to be a great brewer you definitely need to have a grasp of the chemistry but also a feel for the recipe and a genuine love of beer. For that reason, many successful breweries will be run by more than one person, thereby bringing all of these complementary capabilities together to help create the nirvana that is the perfect pint. Ken explains that he will soon have to go and join the board meeting where they will be discussing the five-year business plan. I shiver imperceptibly at these corporate phrases, as memories of my former working life flash across my brain.

They started brewing here in much more modest circumstances in 1997 and I'm informed that the yeast I can see is being used for the 619th time. This is made possible by good husbandry but also the fact that the yeast multiplies while working and so grows in number even after leaving behind some of its vast army of organisms for the secondary fermentation in the cask. The bottling is done offsite so tankers pop along frequently to suck out the equivalent of 150 barrels of beer or about 43,200 pints! Ken informs me that in the old days, before drinking at work became somewhat taboo, the brewers would be given a pint each, every morning and afternoon. These would be delivered by an 'ale laddie', essentially a very welcome variant on the 'tea lady'. If you can't drink on the job in a brewery then something is very wrong with our world today.

Back to camp at Pitlochry where I consume a very large plateful of pasta to provide some inner fuel for what looks like another cold night ahead. Between that, my extra sleeping bag layer and a modicum of cloud cover I pass a relatively temperate night, sleep aided by the Red Rocker and Berserker beers consumed while watching the last two episodes of Series 2 of Only Fools and Horses. Despite my poor brewery hit-rate, it's been a good day thanks to the lovely weather, pretty scenery and Inveralmond Brewery.

It's another fresh, sunny day the next morning and I am untroubled by appointments until 4pm at Kinlochleven. I use the time to plan my trip to Aberdeenshire the next week, where I hope to visit 5 breweries. I call them up one by one but it seems that my losing streak is continuing. The first one is responsive and positive but rarely around as the brewer's day job is in a distillery, so I'm persuaded to give it a miss. The next one is moving premises soon and just can't accommodate visitors right now. One appears to have closed completely after a falling out between the owner and the chef, one's sending its brewers on a course (St Andrew's, Carnoustie…?) and one doesn't ever respond to my calls. Now, I didn't expect plain sailing or red carpets but I am slightly disheartened, especially as this comes on top of several failed attempts to arrange visits with Colonsay and Glenfinnan. I guess it's all part of the rich tapestry that depicts the life of the brewery hunter but I can feel my shoulders sag beneath my sad-puppy face.

With so much free time, I take a stroll through town, stopping for a brisk game of putting on the lovely local course that I once worshipped as a lad. It's wonderfully undulating and you even get a wee scorecard to add a professional touch. I feel an echo of the excitement experienced as a young boy with my dad as my putter is passed through the window and I select my ball. You can have any colour as long as it's white these days whereas I can recall a multitude of colours having been on offer that further added to the sense of occasion. Each hole offers a metal arrow that conveys both the direction and number of the next hole, confirmed by the miniature metal flag. I'm the only one on the course today so it feels like the stage is set for me to indulge in childhood memories while reliving some happy times from long ago. I proceed with needless haste and my putting's even rustier than Brian's chassis. The final hole involves what used to appear like a precipitous downhill slope with a terrifying slant to the right but through adult eyes it seems less scary and I manage to get down in three. I finish one under my easy personal par of 54 but the bloke in the hut's expression confirms just how pathetic an effort this is, registering as 17 over in his book.

I slink into the old 'penny' arcade next door that also held such allure for the junior me and briefly play the 'penny' falls for old time's sake. I inevitably empty my pockets but this is of no concern as the slots here take 2p and 10p pieces so that you can play for longer before losing whatever you came in to spend. The games on offer haven't changed much at all in forty years and I'm delighted to see that the old fashioned horse racing game has survived with its colourful jockeys sliding their steeds toward an uncertain outcome at the beckoning finish line. I take my thoughts and memories for a wander through Pitlochry's main street, resplendent with traditional cafes and retailers of tartan tat but exuding an atmosphere and boasting scenery that still draws the tourists in their droves every year.

Back at camp I suddenly realise that I've been labouring under the misapprehension that Kinlochleven is just an hour away so it's action stations when I discover at 1:30pm that it's actually a drive of two and a half hours! The journey along the A889, A86 and A82 presents Brian and I with some truly stunning scenery and what should have been several excellent photo stops. We speed by the banks of Loch Laggan, resisting the temptation to try out Britain's largest freshwater beach, and hurtle through the pretty villages of Roybridge and Spean Bridge. It's a shame, because days like these are precious in Scotland, but I hate to be late for a date.

Homer seems to have taken us on a most circuitous route and I'm a little surprised to find Fort William hoving into view in front of us, necessitating what feels like a doubling back along the River Leven. I don't mind too much though as I love the views over Loch Linnhe to the Ardnamurchan peninsula, for me the most beautiful, wild and fascinating place in Scotland. The wildlife, isolation, diverse scenery and stunning coastline frequently call upon me to soon return, as I surely will. For now though we must press on and Homer further distinguishes himself when we pass the brewery a full two miles before he's expecting to see it. Harry, the brewer, suggested I call him on arrival as he's at home but there's no signal so I go on a fruitless wander in search of a payphone. This leads me to think that we have been overly keen to rid our streets of these oases of communication, now that we are so deeply into the mobile age. What about having public access mobiles? However, none of this matters as Harry's anticipated the problem and arrives to show me around the brewery.

After being used for aluminium manufacture for many years, these premises housed the Atlas Brewery, which went out of business some time after buying the Orkney Brewery. This led to both being purchased by Sinclair Breweries, moving the Atlas production up to Orkney. Simples. It was from these ashes that Harry built Leven Ales, which he runs himself, carrying out the brewing, cleaning, sales and delivery as well as impromptu tours. Cask ales are brewed with 4% ABV to suit the local tastes whereas the bottles get an extra kick to 4.8%, aimed at the tourist palette. It's pretty spacious and there's a fine view out the window to distract the lonely brewer while he waits for barley to mash or hops to boil. We have a good old natter but I've still got some miles to cover so have to make my excuses. I'm very grateful that Harry's made the special effort to open up, show me around and tell his story and I wish him well for the future.

I'm on my way by 5 o'clock with two bottles of Harry's finest nestling in my well-stocked beer cellar on Brian's port side. I'm hungry and it seems like a long drive up to our camp at Drumnadrochit in the fading light, so I reach for the remaining morsels of my 2-for-1 chocolate oranges purchased earlier in the week. After a couple of hours and a couple of wrong turns I eventually find my home for the night up a steep and twisty farm access road. This is not your common or garden campsite, being a horse stables and riding school, perched on a hill, with a few pitches for campervans round the back. Reception is closed but there's a note inviting me to pitch up and pay in the morning. I'm fairly hungry so get cooking right away but the oil is barely warmed when the gas gives a final cough before breathing its last. I swallow my rising panic into my empty stomach and attempt to administer some form of resuscitation but to no avail. I knew this moment would come of course and have prepared for it by procuring a 3.9kg bottle of propane, the relevant regulator and a jubilee clip. However, I haven't ever attempted this procedure before, it's dark outside and I have no instructions or tools so, having already infused Brian with propane fumes on my first attempt, I decide on another tactic.

The gas bottle is put away as safely as possible and I get down our emergency double-hob electric cooker. This simple appliance consistently overloaded foreign circuits but the British grid is made of sterner stuff and soon my mushroom risotto is on its way. The van is also quite toasty so I take note that an auxiliary heating implement is at hand. After a decent kip I awake to the sight of several lovely horses being led around by their handlers. One gives me an evil stare from his box (a horse not a handler) and one is sporting a haircut so appalling that I have to assume an apprentice horse barber has been let loose, drunk, in the dark. Poor Dobbin. Once the horses have had their morning trot and breakfast hay, the gates are opened and we're on our way. (I really didn't mean for that to rhyme, it's something that happens all the time.) The hour is once more approaching for Brian's weekend sleep before heading off who knows where next week in search of some breweries. My failed attempts at setting up a tour of Aberdeenshire brewing facilities means that I have to hatch an alternative plan before Brian and I are once more reunited in our quest.

This may be as near as you will get

to seeing a horse with a mullet

8 Barley

"You can't be a real country unless you have a beer and an airline. It helps if you have some kind of a football team, or some nuclear weapons, but at the very least you need a beer."

Frank Zappa

Where would we be without barley? More importantly, where would beer be without barley? While you might be able to find a specialist gluten-free beer somewhere out there without a trace of barley, I think I can safely say that beer is made primarily with barley. However wide the cast of ingredients may be, however important the role played by hops, barley will usually have the star billing. Even wheat beers will probably have as much barley in them as wheat. It gives the beer flavour, colour, calories and even foam, but most importantly it provides the sugars for the yeast to ferment into alcohol. So this is the story of barley, from field to firkin, mash tun to cow tum, germination to fermentation.

Before the barley even gets to the brewery it has already been through some pretty unpleasant experiences. After being cut down in its prime it is then threshed (to within an inch of its life), soaked for several days until it sprouts, kilned at temperatures of up to 100° Celsius and beyond, then crushed into grist before its ready for the brewer to use. Why go to such lengths to submit the poor barley to these various forms of serial (or should that be cereal) torture? We need to get our hands on its sugar. The sugars are locked inside the grain in the form of starch and this process is designed to develop the enzymes that will modify the starch into sugars as well as breaking down the proteins into a form that can be used by the yeast. Crushing the grain after it's been kilned, for instance, opens the outer walls to present the sugars more readily. This book isn't about the finer points of cereal husbandry so let's skip the early parts of the process and head for the kiln.

Brewers will talk at length about different types of malt like guitarists will debate the finer points of everything from string selection to pickup position and amp alternatives. I'm not knocking their obsession though (the brewers, not the musos) because few things make more difference to style and flavour than the different varieties of malt. There are many different types of barley that can be grown to start with of course but the kilning process is critical and occurs in two stages – drying then curing. The first stage dries the soaked malt from a moisture content of about 45-50% to about 3-5%, destroying some of the enzymes in the process. By varying the time and temperature during the second stage one can achieve a range of styles and flavours. In simple terms it's akin to adjusting the timer on your toaster depending on how light or dark you want your toast to be. At one end of the scale we have pale malts, which may be used alone to create pale ale but are actually included as a base malt in most beer styles. Higher temperatures or longer periods in the kiln change the colour and taste imparted by the malt and these are consequently added to achieve darker beers such as brown ales, porters and stout. Sniff and savour your pint to detect elements of chocolaty, biscuity, coffee or toffee tones. Crystal malts are something that I came across frequently when visiting breweries and I had assumed that they were just a darker version of pale malt. Turns out however that crystal malt is produced using a special malting process where un-fermentable sugars remain and it can therefore add body, sweetness and mouth feel to a beer. Almost all ales and many lagers have some form of crystal malt in them. The variety of malts available really is quite staggering and brewers will experiment until they achieve the perfect balance in the end product. Getting this right can make the difference between a good beer and a great beer.

Barley, as I mentioned above, may be the star but by no means is it the only player on the stage at this stage. It is extremely common for beers to contain multiple grains and cereals depending on the style and qualities that they are intended to exhibit. Typical examples would include corn, rice, wheat, oats and rye. Wheat, I learned, can help to thicken the head of the beer, making it more appealing visually as well as softening the flavour. The thick head you see on some of the better-known 'smooth' beers is however achieved by the addition of nitrogen. Indeed, that's what the 'widget' in the bottom of a can contains, causing smaller bubbles to form and hence creating a creamier head when the can is opened and the pressure released. Corn and rice are used extensively in large-scale American beers in particular, as these are a cheap way to add sugars and produce a lighter beer. They must love their corn over there (just check out their sense of humour), as it's also the main ingredient in bourbon, unlike our malt whisky that sensibly sticks to barley. To be fair, corn is also a main ingredient in some of the better-known British, Italian and German beers to (not actually) name a few. There are other famous brands that will use lots of sugar or syrup upfront as a cheap means of creating lots of alcohol but fewer carbohydrates. So barley does have some competition in the sugar stakes but it remains the nation's favourite grain in creating our precious pint.

After its long and painful journey from the field, our beloved barley now sits patiently awaiting the next phase of the process. It's already suffered at length for our cause but now it's really getting into hot water. It's time to do the mash. Not the monster mash, just the mash. The malted barley (and any other grains in the mix) is added to the mash tun along with lots of hot water (usually at about 65° C), stirred around a bit then left to infuse. As a rough guide you need 15kg of grain per 100 litres of water to achieve a 5% alcohol beer. The malt is ready and willing to give up its sugars into the warm liquor and after an hour or more we will have a lovely sweet liquid called the wort. This is essentially a barley sugar concoction that probably wasn't the inspiration for Mr Robinson to develop his range of dilutable drinks, so favoured by the Wimbledon set. We really do want to get as much sugar as possible from the mash so to flush out some more, the grains are sparged, essentially sprayed with lots of slightly hotter water. The brewer will calculate how much liquid in total is going to end up in the kettle to control the ultimate alcohol level. As the wort makes it way to the next stage of the brewing process, it's time to say goodbye to our faithful grains as they now exit the brewery to be carted off and used for cow fodder. There are still plenty of nutrients and some sugars left in there so it's not like we've eaten all the chocolates and just left them the marzipan; this is pretty decent scran for our long-lashed ladies in the field. Indeed, the next time you're having a burger with your beer you can ponder how both have been helped on their way by the humble barley grain.

Before we leave the barley topic we should talk a little bit about whisky, proper whisky that is, made in Scotland and known uniquely as Scotch. Everything that happens to the barley in the beer process is essentially replicated for whisky, right up to sending the spent grains to the cows. Where the distiller is seeking to create a whisky that has the peat smoke aromas typical of some island malts, the barley grain will be dried over a peat smoke fire. You could also use that method in making beer (I will try one in the next chapter) but the taste may not appeal to everyone. Malt whisky uses only, or at least predominantly, barley. Grain whiskies, as the name suggests, use different types of grain. Combining the two types of course gives you the blended whiskies that you're allowed to add Coke to. Once the distillery has created the wort it is fermented and then distilled, so one could crudely define whisky as distilled ale. That description perhaps doesn't quite convey the romantic impression of aged malts that is so cleverly crafted by their marketing chaps and I definitely wouldn't mention it within 100 metres of any distillery!

9 Skye

Brian starts at the third attempt – a worrying trend. To be fair he hasn't experienced consistently cold weather like this before and I'm probably not doing him any favours with my clumsy choke control. I've decided to head for Skye this week and see what unfolds in the absence of my intended Aberdeenshire itinerary. The drive takes me across the highlands, past numerous small lochs toward Plockton, on the shores of Loch Carron, and offers some awesome scenery. I note that a few mountains have a dusting of snow on top - a harbinger of winter soon to come. The lochs are so still that they perfectly reflect the undulating hills and trees around them. A couple of fellow campervanners wave as they pass by in their Brians and soon I'm twisting along some lovely single-track roads, exchanging happy greetings with each person making their way back from where I'm going. I love that people still do this, even commercial drivers who must plough along these miniature byways every day of their lives. Perhaps 'toot, wave and smile' appears somewhere in the highland Highway Code, just like the ubiquitous 'mirror, signal, manoeuvre'. Soon we are upon the little village of Plockton and I park Brian by the loch shore so that he can enjoy the view while I go and track down my prey at the Plockton Brewery.

I find Andy's house but there's no sign of Andy, who had earlier invited me to pop round any time. The small shed that houses the brewing kit at the top of the garden is open, so I have a wee look round and take a few photos. I muse over how long it would be before the kit, beer and other goodies were ghosted away if you were to be as trusting in any big city. My spirits are a little low that the week has started with a failure but I know I'll be passing this way again later and feel sure that it'll be second time lucky. My spirits recover quickly in the knowledge that we will soon be arriving on Skye, heralded as one of the most beautiful parts of Scotland, with the jewel of the Cuillin in its crown. Access is simple these days following the controversial construction of the Skye Bridge, which opened in 1995. Tolls of £11.40 return were levied initially to offset the costs of construction, making the crossing fourteen times more expensive than the Forth Road Bridge, although only half its length. Despite this, traffic on the bridge was about 1/3 higher than had been previously recorded on the now defunct ferry. Apparently, local workers for some time gave German vehicles free passage after their team beat England at football. Scottish football, you see, is so poor these days that we often take more pleasure from England losing than Scotland winning. This parochial habit has resulted in sales of foreign football shirts reaching epic proportions whenever the 'Auld Enemy' are involved in a major game.

As we begin to explore the island, it seems like you can see the Cuillin range from almost anywhere and the different angles all betray a fresh wonder. My route takes me around the back road, past the Talisker distillery and on to Dunvegan. The light is beginning to fade as I arrive at my chosen campsite, sitting prettily by the waterside (the campsite, not me). My first task is to connect up the new gas bottle but try as I might I can't get the hose properly on to the bullnose tap that extends from the bottle and the propane is leaking out rapidly. I consult the friendly manager and he advises me to soak the hose in hot water before fitting. This works, but only after various all-in wrestling poses and a great deal of grunting that may be beginning to cause alarm to my fellow campers. My initial elation turns to deflation however when I realise I've forgotten to first loop the jubilee clip over the hose before attaching it. More groans and expletives echo from within Brian as I pull at the hose while holding the bottle between my legs before finally twisting it free. I'm almost exhausted now but find the strength to firmly reattach the hose, with jubilee clip in place and complete the job.

As I'm recovering, my exertions remind me of a scene late one night at a music festival where, both hopelessly drunk, I was trying to get my mate Kevin's wellies off in the mud outside our tent. Either his feet had swollen up or they were at least one size too big to start with, as this was no easy task. We got into a rhythm of manly grunts as we rocked to and fro, desperately trying to gain enough purchase to achieve our goal, culminating in loud sighs of relief when we succeeded with our task. Relief turned to hilarity when we looked around to see several confused and fearful faces staring at us from within the safety of their tents. I think I know what they were thinking but at least we were wearing rubbers.

Gas bottle sorted, I open my bag to find that everything's wet inside. The half empty bottle of water I chucked in there on my way into the plane this morning has leaked due to the pressurisation of the cabin. All of my fresh clothes are soaked and they ain't gonna dry when the temperature's fast approaching zero. Lucky for me the campsite has a dryer and a quick tumble seems to do the trick while I scoff my dinner, ahead of walking into town in search of a pub where I can watch the footie. It's freezing as I stroll into the village and my choice of drinking den seems limited to one, very uninviting, cellar bar where heads turn and conversation ceases as this stranger enters. I nervously order a beer and take a table hidden round the corner but within sight of the box-shaped mini-telly. Predictably Scotland lose 2-0 to Belgium, the beer isn't very good, I'm still not feeling very comfortable and to top my evening off a spaniel jumps into the bar, runs around like mad then selects a spot right next to me to take a dump - definitely time for bed. The walk back is free of street lighting and I'm therefore presented with a sky crammed with stars and a very clear view of the Milky Way. It's Baltic but so beautiful that I have to stand and admire the wonders of our cosmos and forget the little irritations that I might suffer as a mere mortal. It's the coldest night yet in Brian but with my gas heater, electric hob, sleeping bag, quilt and beany, I just about get a decent night's sleep.

The Isle of Skye Brewery is based in Uig at the top end of Skye with great views across to Uist in the Outer Hebrides. The brewery sits next to the ferry terminal from where you can head off to North Uist and Harris and has a well-stocked shop as you enter. In my preparation for this visit, I had noted from their website that tours are neither provided nor encouraged. I feel somewhat honoured therefore when Pam, the head brewer (or more correctly 'brewster'), takes me on an in-depth journey through the brewery's history and potential future. The business started in 1995 when there were a mere dozen or so breweries in Scotland, compared to nearly 70 now. The plant's of a decent size, taking 450kg of grain for each brew. The hops are added in flower form and are handled with gloves to protect from the slightly abrasive oils. Pam's not a fan of hop pellets and I do agree that the natural flowers seem much more in keeping with the art of craft brewing. The mash tun runs at a steady 65 degrees but the cold air outside means that adjustments are sometimes required. Pam shares more about how the business was built but also that the owner, Angus, has been giving serious thought to selling. She explains though that another solution has been found and that I should watch out for a press release in the next few weeks. I'm intrigued but don't feel that I can push for more information so will have to wait and see (as will you).

I advise Pam that I'm off next to the Cuillin Brewery at the Sligachan hotel, which prompts her to tell me her brother is the brewer there, having previously been at Isle of Skye Brewery. I sense the parting wasn't on the happiest of terms and that there may be two quite different versions of the story. Saying no more, Pam kindly furnishes me with 4 bottles from their range and I head back down the main road, stopping briefly in the capital, Portree, for a tasty vegetarian sausage sandwich and cappuccino at the Arriba cafe. I haven't arranged anything with Cuillin but as luck would have it, as I approach, I spot a chap entering what looks like the brewery and he indeed turns out to be Eric, brother of Pam and head brewer here.

We're standing inside the little brewery but any beer talk is shelved as Eric regales me with stories of the sibling rivalry that has ensued over the years following a series of events that unfolded in the manner of a parochial soap opera. It would be wrong for me to share any details here but it did make a change from the usual brewing topics. Eric does find time before I leave to also tell me about what and how he brews, using the slightly peated waters that flow down from the Cuillin. He mostly supplies the hotel but both shut down for the winter and Eric then turns his hand to a variety of building and maintenance tasks. It sounds to me that the sibling relationship needs quite a bit of building and maintenance itself.

Andy at Plockton has rung to say that he was out partying yesterday, (at his grandson's birthday bash), but he's now around if I want to pop by. Pop by I do indeed and in no time we've seen the microbrewery and repaired inside to the warmth to hear Andy's story. Turns out he's an ex Navy man who can't quite recall how he got into brewing. He sells locally and tells me that the water here is so soft he has to add salts to it before it can be used for brewing. He would be happy just to sell locally but demand can vary and so, to sustain his small production line, has started to look further afield. This really is a large scale hobby as much as a small scale business, perhaps more a shed industry than a cottage industry, but size is no indicator of quality and I get the impression that Andy works to high standards. As our discussion draws to a close I remember that I've left Brian's lights on (again) so hurry back to rescue him before planning where to rest our heads this evening. This is one of the joys of the campervan life, being able to choose where to go and where to sleep at a moment's notice. I decide to set Homer's controls for Invergarry near Loch Oich, which sits below Loch Ness. I've selected a campsite that advertises itself as being for 'adults only' and I'm rather intrigued to see what that offers! I arrive as dusk is descending and unfortunately there are no late bars, 18+ movies or other adult-oriented activities, but it's peaceful, childfree and offers excellent Wi-Fi, all for £8.70. I treat myself to a bottle of the Old Worthy ale that is contract brewed at Isle of Skye and boasts whisky peat-smoked barley in its ingredients. It does taste like beer but with the smell and aftertaste of whisky, combining in a very beguiling manner. It's much less cold tonight and with the help of some wine I've bought to vary my beer-oriented diet I sleep long and deep.

The next day is brewery free as unfortunately Glenfinnan aren't around (again) but that gives me the chance to tend to Brian's many needs and treat us to a new hand-held vacuum. In carrying out a full internal clean I take the opportunity to fix his blocked sink. This job calls for the services of Percy the Plunger and a bottle of some foul-smelling liquid that promises to thoroughly clean the gunge from his pipes. Having been plunged and purged, Brian takes us to a campsite not too far from Inverness where we pass an uneventful night before parting briefly ahead of what promises to be an exciting week ahead, visiting the only brewery on an island known globally for its whiskies – Islay.

10 Islay

I'm joined on this week's trek by Greg, an Austrian friend living in
London, who has given up a week of his hard earned holiday to ride
with Brian, see Islay (pronounced 'eye la', not 'eye lay') and enjoy a
few beers. Our plane's an hour late as we arrive at Inverness to pick up
the ever-patient Brian. Yes, Glasgow airport would have been much
closer but that's not where I'd left Brian. We head south, stopping
briefly at Urquhart Castle on the shores of Loch Ness for some photos,
before continuing down past Fort William and through Glencoe. I am
both thrilled and humbled by the power and majesty of the Glencoe
mountain range and the raw spirit of the landscape. I try to drive really
slowly, taking in every curve, swoop and precipitous edge of the
magnificent topography opening up before us.

I find myself reflecting that this was once home to the
MacDonalds, who suffered the infamous massacre on the orders of
King William II in 1692. The echoes of that evil deed still somehow
pervade the atmosphere of these wild lands today. Survivors did later
return to settle here once more and, despite their possessions and
property having been lost, they clung with passion to their harsh life.
As these thoughts are occupying my mind we see ahead an imperious
stag, antlers held high, standing perfectly still atop a mound, proudly
scanning his territory. I almost drive off the road, suddenly feeling

rather insignificant, as I stare in awe at this iconic vision. We continue on through Rannoch Moor, its other-worldly moonscape of scattered, dead trees and shallow pools, presenting the most uninviting of environments for any poor soul finding themselves stranded here. I check Brian's instruments and squeeze a little harder on the accelerator…

Our late start, my optimistic time estimates and nights that are definitely drawing in mean that darkness is falling as we make our way toward Inverary where we plan to camp for the night. It's getting harder to see the road ahead clearly due to Brian's inadequate headlights. Greg's somewhat concerned and with his prompting and some trial and error I learn that what was Brian's full-beam switch is now his dipped setting. The old dipped setting is now essentially sidelights only, except Brian has no such thing, which explains the poor visibility we've been suffering. These changes were part of the surgery he underwent to make him fit for service in the UK and this is the first time I've discovered them! As it gets even darker and we twist our way through the blackness, I'm wishing Brian had a full beam setting. "Maybe he does", says Greg. "Try pulling back the indicator." "No, that doesn't wo……ah, yes it does."

Happily engaged with Brian's newly found light show capabilities I suggest some music and Greg makes an excellent choice in Veruca Salt's album, American Thighs. Lighter of heart as we sense our destination nearing, we decide that if the campsite doesn't have a restaurant we're heading back to town to find a hotel bed. At the third attempt we find the entrance to the campsite, locate the manager and enquire after their restaurant situation. Well, this bloke has probably never seen such elation displayed from campers on hearing that the campsite refreshment facilities are closed. We have our excuse, it's been a very long day and it's with almost no shame whatsoever that we retreat to town, check in to the Argyll Hotel and stroll round the corner to enjoy a fine dinner at the George, washed down with a couple of pints of Hurricane Jack. Back at the Argyll we feel it would be rude not to buy some drinks from the lone waitress/receptionist and we eventually persuade her to join us in the empty bar. She's new here and we obviously did nothing to enhance her promotion prospects, as her manager later admonishes her for socialising with the punters. We eventually retire (collapse) about 1am, fully satisfied with our day's 'work'.

Our first stop next morning is the Fyne Ales Brewery (makers of the aforementioned Hurricane Jack), at the top of Loch Fyne, down the end of an old farm road. We're a tad early but we amuse ourselves by photographing the highland cattle as they observe us through their ultra cool fringes. Folk start to arrive but none are approaching us with a smile of recognition so I go in search of the lady I'd spoken to a few days before. I succeed in finding the wrong lady who then passes us over to a bloke who chats away very amiably before it dawns on me that he has absolutely no idea who we are or why we're here. I interrupt our conversation for him to confirm that he indeed knows nothing of our visit and to advise that our expected contact Chris has gone home after completing a nightshift. However, without missing a beat, Malcolm kindly agrees to show us around.

It's a ten-barrel set-up here but with plans for some serious expansion. We engage in a bout of hop smelling and Malcolm explains how the scent varies by country of origin - fruity, spicy or citrus tones that you can mix and match to get just the effect you're after. I'm very excited to see that the wort is flowing from the mash tun and the sparging arm is in full flow. I've never yet seen this in action and Malcolm explains that the temperature is a few degrees higher for this phase of the brew to drive out more sugars from the grain.

We get to talking about the German quality standard, the Reinheitsgebot, and its consequent impact on the quality of the beers brewed within its requirements. Malcolm then offers a further insight into an unintended consequence of limiting the art of brewing to barley, hops, water and yeast. To find flavours not available through other forbidden, added ingredients, the Germans have developed an incredible palette of barley malts, offering a range of tastes not typically available elsewhere. Consequently Fyne Ales will often make a shopping trip there to enhance their barley store. We also chat about the industry in Scotland, which Malcolm proudly proclaims to have "not many a**eholes" thus making it a rewarding place to work. We note that the name of the brewery clearly offers an easy pun and is often mistaken for an attempt at an Olde English spelling of 'fine ales', which can't be a bad thing.

It's only 10am and already we've done half of our work for the day with only one other brewery to see. To get there we need to catch the ferry from Kennacraig, at the northern end of Kintyre, to Port Askaig on Islay, the spiritual home of malt whisky. The Caledonian MacBrayne vessel we board appears brand new in terms of its spotless appearance but about 30 years old in terms of its décor, including a bizarre centrepiece made up of umpteen shards of colourful plastic, or was it kryptonite? We learn later that it was built in Poland in 2011, which might explain both of our apparently incongruous observations. We explore the ship, making sure we have experienced every deck from bow to stern and taken in the gorgeous views that surround us. We concur that it's time for lunch now that our capacious breakfasts have fought their way closer to their ultimate destination. The restaurant we choose is small, the staff are friendly and we are informed that all the food is freshly prepared. I order a surprisingly decent macaroni cheese and chips while Greg selects the fish and chips. His demolition of the grub is paused only to profess a string of superlatives, ultimately declaring that this may be the best fish and chips he has ever devoured. This is an opinion that will be shared with most of the folk we meet over the next two days.

I steer Brian off the ship and set a course for our second brewery of the day and the only one on this island. Steve is manning the Islay Brewery shop out front while Paul is busy in the brew house next door. The latter explains the genesis of setting up a brewery on an island known globally for its whiskies. In essence a germ of an idea discussed over a few beers came to life upon a chance meeting with a third party who knew about brewing and that was the catalyst that converted idea to reality. The intention was to supply hostelries on the island and indeed 90% of all production is consumed without adding to the ferry's freight weight. As we learned earlier, making whisky or beer starts in much the same way, which means the wash (wort) from the distillery up the road can be used to then make beer. Similarities in the process end there though as, while Paul brews the sweet liquid with hops, producing beer in a few days, the chaps up the road distil it slowly and we have to wait several years to taste the fruits.

I have been labouring under the misapprehension for most of my life that the peaty aroma/flavour in whiskies is imparted from the peatyness within the water used to make the whisky. This, I learn, is in fact not the case at all. The familiar peat smoke tones are imparted by smoking the barley over a peat fire. I would like to apologise unreservedly for my stupidity. There is no doubt that the quality and nature of the water does affect the character of any given whisky but the peatyness comes from the smoking. I suggest to Paul that therefore there is no reason why you couldn't make a whisky with Islay characteristics outside of Islay. He agreed but suggested that I might not want to say too much about that while on the island.

Duties fulfilled, we're planning on a long walk the next day so head to Bowmore to check out the Tourist Information office. It's due to close at 5 but when we arrive at 4 it's already locked up. Islanders eh? So, we head to Port Charlotte where we plan to camp the night. Planning and execution are distant cousins at times so we check out the local hostel (closed), the posher hotel (£120 a night – 'normally £180' we are informed) and the less posh option that is apparently full.

Thus thwarted we head for the camp, which, for all intents and purposes, presents itself as offering excellent football facilities but little else. Indeed, were it not for the sole campervan lined up by the front we'd have assumed we were in the wrong place. Uninspired by what we've seen and clocking the significant hike required from pitch (camping not football) to ablution facilities, we sheepishly sneak off to check out sleeping options in Bowmore.

On arrival we notice that the Tourist Info office is now occupied despite it having gone 5. Making up for lost time no doubt. We present our best 'lost, needy tourists' look, smiling inanely at the lady within, silently mouthing "open?" to which she silently mouths "no" with a gentle, but final, shake of the head. Unperturbed we tour around the bed choices, which prove to be closed, expensive, weird or just unwilling to answer the bell. We also note with dismay that the local bistro, a major draw in seeking accommodation in Bowmore is… closed! This is not going well.

It is with heavy hearts and lead-like limbs that we climb back into Brian, tails between legs, and head once more for the campsite. It's dark now and we could murder a beer so we pitch up briskly and make our way to the Port Charlotte hotel where we indulge in a well-earned three-course meal, a few beers and several whiskies. Greg bravely experiments with the local firewater, preferring the smokier Laphroaig to the sharper tones of the Bowmore, but promising to attempt all eight brands whilst in 'Rome'. We sleep deeply and warmly in Brian, the elements providing a very comfortable, still, almost balmy 10°

Celsius overnight.

The next morning we're keen to do the walk, not least to shed a few of the pounds we've gained so far this week. Tracy the barmaid gave us a hot tip on where to go but it's less than clear exactly where the path starts so we instead drive to the finishing point and work backwards. On the way we pass the newest distillery on Islay, Kilchoman, and a ruined church that we hope marks the start of the trail. After aborting several promising pathways we're still at the church so we decide to instead traverse the long, sandy beach nearby before climbing up and over a hill past what appears to be marauding gangs of sheep, menacingly approaching us in a pincer movement. We hold our nerve until, turning a corner, we are confronted by a group of highland cattle, whose fringes give them the same menacing appearance achieved by thugs wearing hoodies. Even although we can't see their eyes, they win the staring contest and we retreat back to Brian.

We stop off at the Kilchoman distillery for a rather delicious lunch, topped off with lemon drizzle cake soaked in 'new make'. They can't call this alcoholic liquid 'whisky' yet as it comes direct from the still and has not matured for long enough to earn that accolade. For the record, it really doesn't taste very nice and somewhat ruined what had clearly once been a rather pleasant cake. We've decided to stay tonight at Port Ellen at the south of the island so that we can maximise our sleep prior to boarding the ferry there in the morning. Port Ellen boasts three distilleries lined up east of the village; Ardbeg, Lagavulin and Laphroaig. These three produce intense whiskies, saturated with peat-smoke, brine and iodine. We visit all three, Greg purchasing some samples from each, before returning to check out the accommodation options. We should have learned by now to book in advance as we are met with 'no vacancies' everywhere we try. Eventually we find a place that offers us their backyard for Brian at just £5 for the night, which is very cheap but has limited appeal. We're saved from this Spartan sleeping arrangement by the last bed in the village. It's semi en-suite with a separate loo and a Perspex cuboid in the corner of the room, masquerading as a shower. There's no curtain and therefore no modesty, but we figure we'll figure it out. Beer time!

You meet the most interesting people in the smallest places. The larger the town or city the more anonymous that people remain. Chuck a bunch of strangers in a tiny outpost like Port Ellen though and everyone wants to chat. We spend some time with the ebullient Canadian Shirley and daughter Katie who are occupying the proper en-suite at our B&B. We get chatting to an English bloke who seems to spend most of his time island hopping to work on communication masts for the BBC and local coastguards. Then there was the very drunk and loud Patrick from Eton whom poor Greg got stuck with. Another serious amount of food, beer and whisky is then followed by a deep sleep in very comfortable beds before we have to deal with the slightly uncomfortable matter of the showers. I volunteer to go first on condition that Greg remains buried under his covers and facing the wall. In the spirit of friendship I then take a walk around the village after getting dressed, while Greg freshens up. I can detect that we are speaking in slightly deeper voices and walking in a very mannish way as we make our way to breakfast.

The same ferry that brought us over takes us back to the mainland and, as we chill, Greg reveals the life-changing revelation that has, er, revealed itself to him during this trip. He's noticed that despite consuming industrial quantities of beer every night, he has awoken tired, but headache free. No hangover at all. He attributes this to the quality ingredients and complete absence of nasty additives in the craft beers and real ales. Indeed he wonders why, when he demands exactly those qualities from his food, he's never thought to demand the same from his alcohol. He also realises that he can get trolleyed more often without fear of losing the next day curled up in bed with a mug of chicken soup (his preferred cure). This paradigm shift in Greg's alcohol strategy makes the whole trip seem all the more worthwhile.

We break our journey to Inverness at Oban and Banavie, where we explore the wonder that is Neptune's Staircase, a series of eight locks on the Caledonian Canal, lifting (or dropping) boats by 20 metres. It's still rather chilly so we quickly re-join Brian and before long we've left the length of Loch Ness behind us and are securing a room in downtown Inverness before heading off to once more do our duty in sampling the pleasures on offer. These include excellent pizzas, more fab local craft beers, a few whiskies and a fine musical performance (not by us obviously) late at night in the Market bar. Sleep once more comes easily and we take a brisk and bracing walk through town before repairing to the airport. Just before we say goodbye to Greg though he earns himself a shiny gold star for his quick thinking and lightning reflexes. I had parked Brian in a space, got distracted and failed to notice that we were gently slipping backwards until I heard Greg cry "brake, brake", which I heard as "break, break" and therefore froze in a moment of confusion. Greg's critical dive and athletic twist enabled him to pull on the handbrake just feet short of a very shiny and expensive looking Mercedes that we were accelerating towards. Poor Brian, I felt guilty for days after.

A wild and dangerous beast

11 Hops

"He was a wise man who invented beer."

Plato

Scotland is a hopless country. That's not a typo of course; as this is a book about Scotland and beer I just wanted to begin this section by making the point that it is extremely difficult to grow hops in Scotland due to the climate. Despite this fact, hops have been used in Scotland for at least two hundred years, although in some more remote areas they probably continued to use other bittering herbs such as heather, broom and myrtle for some while longer. Indeed, the Williams Brothers Brewery presently markets Fraoch Ale that uses heather rather than hops for flavour and bitterness. One beer expert did tell me that 'ale' was actually the term used for beer without hops and 'beer' by definition is made with hops. I believe that he is absolutely correct historically, but given that CAMRA are very much including hopped beers in their definition of real ale, I think we can use the terms quite interchangeably. For me personally, I always call stuff coming out of a tap from a keg, 'beer', and stuff coming out of a pump from a cask, 'ale'. Or would you say that ale is a subset of beer along with all other styles such as lager or stout? Perhaps a topic to debate over a pint one evening I would suggest. How did I get on to the difference between beer and ale? Oh yeah, hops!

Hops are grown in many places across the world and with modern distribution methods they can all be made available to brewers in Scotland or elsewhere. The country with the highest level of hop production is Germany, closely followed by the USA. The Czech Republic, Slovenia and New Zealand are other places that I frequently heard mentioned as hop sources for brewers. Why trouble to import hops from these places when there's a plentiful supply growing in England? It is simply because there is such a plethora of varieties available from different countries, offering an even wider palette of flavours to help us create signature beers. From America we find the three famous Cs among the staggering variety of hops they offer, those being Cascade, Centennial and Columbus, marked out predominantly by their citrus tones. From England we have Brewer's Gold that is described as resiny/spicy, Challenger that offers marmalade/toffee elements or Goldings that adds a smooth/sweet flavour. German hop varieties can be floral, fruity or citrus with the popular Saaz being described as cinnamon spicy and earthy. I could go on and on but I'm sure you can already appreciate how beer tasting sessions can be just as full of superlatives and adjectives as any wine or whisky tasting.

Why do we add hops to beer in the first place? Essentially for two reasons, bitterness and aroma. I mention them in that order because that's the order in which they are added to the wort in the kettle. Hops selected because they are effective at imparting bitterness are added near the start of the boil and those that offer aromas are chucked in nearer the end. Bittering hops tend to have more 'Alpha' acids while aroma hops have more 'Beta'. These wonderful plants also operate as a preservative, help to improve the foam on the beer and act as an anti-bacterial agent. No wonder they're one of the three theological virtues - Faith, Hops and Charity. When I first saw hops being added by a brewer I was struck by the very small amounts that are added. You may recall that 15kg of barley is added per 100 litres of liquor. The equivalent amount of hops is just 70g. That's one part hops for 200 parts barley! Flower power.

Hops look a little bit like small, green pinecones and grow very tall with the help of wires that they can climb up. Their long stems are called bines, which sound to me a bit like how a Spanish person would pronounce 'vines'. A bine however differs from a vine not only in pronunciation but also in its method of climbing. A bine apparently climbs by its shoots growing in a helix around a support whereas a vine climbs using tendrils or suckers. So now you know! As is so often the case with nature it's the females that deliver the goods. Only female hops are grown for beer purposes and they're harvested in autumn before being dried and baled for delivery to brewers around the globe. One of my favourite hop stories that my research unearthed described how hops were once noted to produce early menstruation periods in women who worked in the fields. This is apparently because hops are one of the most oestrogenic plants on earth. Even better, the actual substance they contain is oestrogen estradiol, which has been proven to reduce testosterone levels in men. Could this be the explanation for brewers' droop?

So, let us continue along the beer production line, having previously sent the sweet wort on its sweet way to the kettle, where it is boiled before adding the hops at two different stages. This can also be an opportunity to add other flavourings or ingredients and really there seems to be no limit to what these crafty brewers lob in. Chocolate, fruit, spices, honey, treacle, pepper, chilli, coffee, mustard, bacon and even oysters have all been included, but perhaps not together. I have tasted a couple of very nice beers with coffee included, one example of which is called Brewed Awakening (what is it with brewers and puns?), made by Cromarty. I don't have much of a problem with honey or even treacle and wouldn't say no to chocolate in anything but I do think most of these sound like a triumph of imagination over inspiration and would much prefer just to drink really excellent beer-flavoured beer.

I was once in Budapest with a friend (Kevin of wellie grunting fame) and we fancied an ice cream so we asked the young lady what flavours she had. She replied, "vanilla, chocolate, strawberry, caramel, beer, mint…" at which point we jumped in and said "beer, really, you have beer flavoured ice cream?" In a very nonchalant manner she confirmed that not only did she have beer ice cream, but also that it was one of their most popular flavours. So, curiosity running wild, we purchased one each and tucked in. We were trying very hard to taste the beer but it just wasn't coming through. If anything there was a slight apple flavour maybe? Then it hit us – she didn't say beer ice cream, she said "pear" ice cream with a slightly Hungarian accent.

What a let down, but we ate them anyway.

Once the boil in the kettle is done, the very hot liquid is cooled and sent off to the fermentation vats where the yeast will be added. This cooling happens on the way to the vats by means of a cunning little device called a heat exchanger. I'm always amazed by how small these often are when they have to cool fairly vast quantities of liquid from 100C to around 20C. The spent hop flowers act as a filtration bed so that the liquid leaving the kettle leaves behind the gunk that has accumulated during the boil. Where the brewer uses pellets, this method doesn't work and instead they may use a whirlpool to isolate the unwanted pellet particles. Some of the big brand brewers apparently use hop oils instead of pellets or flowers, which just seems like cheating. Sometimes brewers will add hops after the primary fermentation or even into the cask itself, to add some further delicate hop aromas. This is known as dry hopping and can also be done by adding hops to something called a hop-back that sits between the kettle and fermentation vats. If there's a hundred ways to do something, brewers will quickly find a hundred more I've learned. Anyway, I think I'm getting a bit hopped out now so let's re-join Brian.

12 Bonnie Dundee

I'm delighted to discover that the EasyJet winter timetable has shifted the departure time for the morning flight from Luton to an hour and a quarter later, allowing me a more civilised hour at which to rise. After five weeks of exploring the highlands and islands, it's time to head further south to discover the breweries that lie closer to Scotland's central lowlands. I'm curious to find out how these might differ from their country cousins and to learn more about the history of Scottish brewing, which had its epicentres in Glasgow, Alloa and Edinburgh. The flight's on time so I have an afternoon to make my way to Dundee where I'll be staying over with mum and dad.

Brian coughs into life with a puff of blue smoke and Homer leads us on a series of twisty single-track roads that soon take us past Cawdor, famous from the 'Scottish play', Macbeth, who of course was Thane of Cawdor before becoming King of Scotland. Apparently the village and castle were actually called Calder originally but the name was changed in the 19th century to match the Shakespearean spelling, such is the power of the pen. We drive on past Grantown on Spey and through the Cairngorm National Park, looking naked and self-conscious without its winter covering of snow. The many chairlifts creak and sway as they slumber through their summer hibernation. The scene that unfolds before us presents desolate, undulating moorland stretching in every direction.

As we make our way through the wilderness, I'm desperately seeking a quiet spot where I can recycle all the water I've been drinking, but nowhere meets the criteria of dry, accessible and out of sight. My discomfort pricks my conscience as I recall that poor Brian's bladder hasn't been emptied in some time. That adds a fourth criterion – 'suitable for draining Brian's grey water container' (aka bladder). After a couple of false hopes are dashed we find the perfect spot and sigh in unison as we do what nature intended. We're both a bit happier and Brian a touch lighter as we speed on our way. I soon see signs for Fettercairn and I'm reminded of my student days in Dundee where a friend, who had once earned the much sought after title of Miss Fettercairn, insisted that we have a night out in the nearby metropolis of Brechin at a club that I think was called the Steakhouse. Well, it was more like a Hothouse that night as all I can remember is watching the rivulets of sweat pouring down the walls while drunken teuchters marauded around the dance floor.

On the way down to Dundee I stop off at Burnside Brewery in Laurencekirk where I meet with brothers Dave and Gary. It's a 9-barrel plant that started in 2010 and apart from the three fermenters, Dave has built the rest of the kit himself. I'm drawn to the wort basin or underback where the sweet wort whirls around before making its way to the copper. The swirling motion causes any unwanted particles to fall to the bottom and gather in the middle of the basin, so that the liquid passed on is pure and uncluttered. This phenomenon is called the 'Tea Leaf Paradox' and none other than Alfred Einstein eventually explained it. The TLP refers to the way that tea leaves cluster in the middle of the bottom of a teacup when the liquid is stirred, when you might intuitively expect them to be dispersed up and out by the same forces acting on the liquid. I'm not going to attempt the full scientific explanation of this phenomenon but essentially it goes something like this: the outward forces (centrifugal) are offset by hitting the walls of the cup, creating an opposing force (centripetal) that pushes the tea leaves down. They stay there because they're too heavy to be lifted back up by the rotating forces. I bet you're wondering how you could ever have enjoyed a cup of tea without knowing that information but it does at least help to explain the title of this book, which explores its own paradox i.e. discovering 'beer' in the land of 'whisky'.

Dave and Gary have been excellent hosts but they've got stuff to do and places to be as well as preparing for the visit of 50 odd squaddies the next day. (I should have hyphenated '50 odd' to clarify my meaning there.) Gary kindly loads me up with two bottles each of their 4 varieties, which I gently store atop my growing mound of delicious beers. The clocks moved back at the weekend so the light is already fading and there's still a bit to go to get to the City of Discovery, my hometown. The City of Discovery tag refers to Captain Scott's ship that was built in Dundee and now acts as its signature tourist attraction. In my ignorance I had always glibly associated Scott and the Discovery with the conquest of the South Pole. Actually, Discovery was used for earlier research in the Antarctic and another ship, Terra Nova, took Scott and his team on the conquest. They did get there but only after a team of Norwegians beat them to it and sadly

Scott and his men all died on the return journey. Still, should you find yourself in Dundee, the ship is quite stunning to behold.

Growing up, Dundee was known as the city of jute, jam and journalism. In the late 19th century the jute industry employed over 30,000 people in 60 mills across Dundee, but that industry now no longer exists. The 'jam' really refers to marmalade but was generalised to afford the handy alliteration. This relates in particular to the Keiller factory that is apocryphally credited with inventing marmalade but did at least industrialise its production. They opened an operation in North Woolwich in 1879, where my great grandfather once worked before moving to Dundee, following a promotion. This ultimately led to me being a Dundonian rather than a Londoner, but I have now forgiven him and returned to the city he left all those years ago. The journalism piece of course refers to D C Thomson Ltd, who publish such titles as The Sunday Post, The Beano and, until recently, The Dandy. This is the only one of the three J's remaining in Dundee today but without much of its former glory.

While enjoying a fine location on the banks of the River Tay, Dundee is not known as a popular tourist destination – indeed it was once reported as the third least visited place after Bradford and Wakefield. Presumably the visitors it does get, mostly come from those two places. I was however surprised to learn that it is twinned with Dubai, an honour shared by the likes of Milan, Barcelona and Rio de Janiero. The only vague connection between Dubai and Dundee that I can come up with is that supporters of Dundee United Football

Club are known as Arabs, which may have caught the attention of some footie fan Sheikh in Dubai. In case you're wondering, we (yep, I'm a United fan) got that moniker apparently because there used to be a sand running track around the pitch and the swirling wind would often cause a mini sandstorm where the fans were standing, therefore making them look like a bunch of 'Arabs'. There is more than a sporting chance that this story is also entirely apocryphal though!

We arrive at my parents' place and Brian is given the sort of warm welcome you'd expect for a special family member. I leave him perched half on the pavement to offset the significant camber and pop inside for chow and chat. A half decent microwave curry precedes the slow torture that is watching Dundee United lose on penalties to Hearts in the League Cup on telly. A couple of samples from my beer cellar keep me in good spirits however, before kipping in the attic ahead of my next day's labours. First stop is Angus Ales up in Carnoustie (or Car'snooty' as we used to call it. Almost anywhere near Dundee that wasn't Dundee was considered posh.) The town is of course famous for its links golf course and Alan has named his beers in honour of the sport, Mashie Niblick being an example. The brewery, like many I've seen, is housed in a simple industrial unit; fit for purpose but not pretty. Alan explains that he prefers to use plastic casks as "the neds steal the metal ones" to sell for scrap - empty, I assume. Alan expresses a 'realistic' (aka grim) view of the state of the ale market for small breweries that are trying to compete with the bigger players. I understand the points he's making but it's the first time I've heard a less than positive view. Certainly, local trade is important for small breweries and as Alan says "Edinburgh likes ale,

Dundee doesn't".

The question of whether the recent expansion of craft breweries can be sustained or whether consolidation is inevitable is a topic that I shall engage more than once in this book. My observations to date lead me to believe that, unless your objectives are very modest, you need at least a 10 or 20 barrel plant, investment, marketing, some differentiation and ultimately perhaps your own retail outlet. Retail does seem to be king whether you're making beer, beans or bacon. (What an explosive combination that would be!) The English market is crowded and while overseas sales offer opportunity, exporting brings its own challenges. Many of the brewers I spoke to fear that saturation point isn't far away and there are several successful mid-size breweries well positioned to take up any slack in the market. On that subject, it turns out that the news of which Pam in Skye had forewarned me has become public. The Isle of Skye brewery is to merge with the Isle of Arran Brewery under the holding company, Arran Brewery plc. Their joint efforts will apparently produce around 500,000 litres of beer each year but plans for far greater expansion have been hinted at. Indeed, it is later announced that Arran are also to buy a former distillery near Falkirk to turn into a craft brewery and visitor centre. I doubt if this will be the last news of this sort in the years to come.

A short trip up the road takes me to Mor Brewery (pronounced 'More', a Gaelic word meaning great or big). Jim's the brewer here, a former RNLI man, and he tells me about his modest 2.5 BBL (barrel) plant, tucked away in his back garden – less is Mor I guess. One brewing run provides about 8 casks, which is enough to meet the demand from his customers but short of the 4 BBL capacity that he reckons you need to "make a living". It's a labour of love for Jim though and he does have some other income to keep the wolf from the door. We chew the fat over a cuppa, talk about other local brewers and then make a very brief visit to the brewery itself. Before I depart we swap campervan tales when I notice the rotting carcass of an old VW in his garden. For Jim this clearly remains a future project fuelled by dreams of long, sunny camping trips, but one day perhaps the campervan will be restored and it will be the brewery that's left to crumble.

Back at the ranch I give Brian a thorough clean up, inside and out, ahead of his long awaited photo opportunity with mum and dad perched inside. They clamber in pretty smoothly for folk in their eighties and look every bit the part with Dad behind the wheel and mum occupying the passenger seat. Brian's been pretty busy for the last 6 weeks so he's getting a week's holiday with his grandparents while I go and move house in London. We will then spend a month together (me and Brian, not me and my parents) exploring Fife and Stirlingshire, the Lothians and Borders before Christmas comes and winter really sets in.

13   St Andrews to Bo'ness

Brian's looking well rested, sparkly clean and has no doubt been the subject of much love and admiration from my parents while I've been away over the last week. As if to confirm his state of wellbeing he starts first time with barely a puff of smoke. We're off today to see the Eden Brewery, which is based in Guardbridge near St. Andrews, professes historical and other links to St Andrews, features the name St Andrews on one of its beers but isn't the St Andrews Brewery, which is based in Glenrothes, which is some distance from St Andrews. Hopefully that was entirely clear and if you're not already fed up with St Andrews, you can read more about that brewery later.

It's only natural that St Andrews should have all of this attention foisted upon it. A beautiful wee town on the Fife coast that is not only known as the global home of golf but also the site of Scotland's first university and the oldest in the UK outside of Oxford and Cambridge. Indeed Glasgow, Aberdeen and Edinburgh all followed St Andrews before the 'modern' universities of the 18th century started to appear across England. The fame and prestige of St Andrews was further enhanced of course when it provided the stage upon which the relationship between Prince William and Kate Middleton (no relation, unfortunately) began. So you can see why one might crave to demonstrate some allegiance with the name.

The Eden Brewery is based at the old Guardbridge Paper mill and has been in production only a couple of months when I meet the man in charge, Paul Miller. Paul explains that this is the first time a brewery has been based here for 110 years but at one time nearly 100 people were employed in brewing in the St Andrews area. He shows me some papers from 1878 demonstrating that beer at that time was sold at 6d per gallon, or 2.5p in new money. At one time the Haig family, Scotland's oldest whisky dynasty, also had a distillery at this site and farmed their own barley at Daftmill farm down the road, so called because the stream looks like it's flowing uphill - even when sober.

Paul is experimenting with maturing the beer in barrels that have been used for wines such as Sauterne as well as whiskies like Ballechin. When the same barrel has housed both wine and whisky the beer takes on the aromas and flavours of both. Concoctions like these may even coax the inveterate wine snob to seriously consider craft beers as a viable alternative. These lend themselves to being drunk over dinner with guests who can wax lyrical about the nose, the notes, the aftertaste and how certain foods are best matched with one beer or another. The incredible variation of grains, hops and other miscellaneous ingredients together with the many styles of brewing and even the type of water used, together offer beer-buffs endless hours of palate drenching debate. If the growth of craft beers is to continue then attracting new followers from the dinner party darlings will be almost as important as converting the seasoned lager drinkers over to a hoppy IPA. Craft beers will never be as big as branded lagers in sales but they could maybe be seen as a creative 'Apple' to the mass-produced 'Microsoft' beers.

The next day I have two afternoon appointments so decide to swing by Kirkcaldy in the morning, hoping to be able to pop in to see the microbrewery in one of the pubs down there. The place looks closed apart from a wee Scottie dog staring back at me through the window so I decide just to take a photo and seek out a coffee. As I walk away a lady comes running up behind me wondering why I was photographing her bar, so I explain and we go inside. She's busy on a call that gives me time to properly engage my brain and remember that the pub I'm seeking is called the Harbour Bar, which this one isn't. I feel that I can't just leave so I wait until she's done before making my red-faced apology. I walk further down the road and soon find my prey. It's looking even more closed – not even a wee dog anywhere in sight. So, I re-enact my photo/leave/coffee routine and feeling a little guilty, half-tick the Fyfe Brewery off my list with a light pencil. I might well return at some point but I had been told that they weren't brewing right now anyway so one must live with these difficult, professional decisions.

I have an appointment with Harviestoun in Alva near Alloa, a hub of historical brewing in Scotland. George Younger was encouraged to set up his business in this area long ago due to the good water supplies and the availability of barley from the carselands nearby. I'm a bit early so I huddle up against the cold in Brian and munch my egg sandwich. The appointed hour arrives and I meet Stuart who explains the origins of the brewery and the reason behind the harvest mouse on their logo. Apparently the founder, Ken Brooker, would see this wee creature scurrying about in the early days and as it seemed like he was sharing its space, it became the poster rodent for the brewery. One of the beers by the way, Bitter & Twisted, was apparently named after Ken by his wife – reports that Loving & Handsome came a close second cannot be confirmed.

We chat about contract brewing (where an established brewery produces beer for a 'cuckoo' brewer), which always strikes me as a convenient but sub-optimal arrangement for both parties, except maybe as a temporary arrangement. It just seems to me that a brewer, his brewery and his beers should all co-exist or you risk losing some of the character and soul of the final product. A chef wouldn't get someone else to cook his food in another kitchen, although as restaurants become chains I guess that does happen in a way, often to the detriment of the original quality. Stuart has another reason for not contract brewing in that breweries making less than 5,000 hectolitres per annum (or c60 barrels a week) benefit from a halving of beer duty, tapering up to a maximum of 60,000 hectolitres per annum. This was great news when introduced by Gordon Brown in 2002 but since then the industry has had to deal with the 'duty escalator', which presently increases duty at 2% above inflation every year, thus making beer production more and more expensive at a time when people want to pay less and less. The demand for cheap, quality beer at point of sale is perhaps best demonstrated by the Wetherspoon chain that delivers exactly what the pennywise customer wants but at a price to the brewer that can exclude all but the scale players. I reckon though that this chain should be nationalised to provide a halfway house between old folk living at home and going into care. It's warm and safe, the staff are nice, the food's cheap and the beers are good. Sorted!

Harviestoun is one of the larger Scottish independent breweries and actually has more sales in England than Scotland. Nearly half of these sales are in casks with kegs at just 15% but growing and the rest is in bottles. About 20% of these bottles meet the lips of their end user outside of these fine isles. I've tasted their draught Schiehallion before, which has a hoppy, grapefruit flavour and Stuart explains that demand for hoppier beers is growing in Scotland – a departure from our typical preference for maltier, sweeter beers compared to our cousins down south where 'bitter' is very much the preferred style. Before I go we have a look round the premises and I see the contraption that weighs then delivers the grain blend to the mash tun. Apparently this piece of kit can also be used to deliver chicken feed to hungry hens, but is being put to a much more noble use here.

My next appointment takes me back across Fife to Glenrothes where St Andrew's Ales are based in a small industrial unit. As I mentioned earlier, more than one brewery professes links (ha ha, golf pun) to St Andrews. However, Bob has the name and although he's 20 miles away it's a very valuable commodity and there's every chance that he might one day find premises within the grand old town itself. Bob's no stranger to beer writing as well as beer, having toured round the breweries of Idaho one time and published a guide. Sounds like a great idea! He's been brewing here since January, focusing on bottles and finding retail outlets for his range of seven regular and three 'guest' beers. I discover that the secondary fermentation in the bottle is primed by adding a little sugar for the yeasty beasties to munch on. This ensures that the beer remains 'real' and alive right up to when it begins its final journey through whichever lucky human has acquired that privilege. Bob intends to make the most of his marketing edge and already his beers retail in many smart outlets. He kindly furnishes me with a three-bottle presentation pack before I head off west again toward Bridge of Allan.

The Tin-Pot Brewery sits within the Allanwater Brewhouse and Pub, hidden behind a curtain that could as easily have been hiding a small stage. Actually, let's hold on to that image of the stage because making beer in this little space has elements of drama, a touch of comedy but thankfully no tragedies. The main player on this stage, the leading man if you will, is Douglas Ross. I meet him in the bar area to the front where 'audiences' gather to try some of the eight brews on offer, proudly displaying their evocative names such as Bramble Pot, Hop Nouveau and even Sticky Toffee Pudding. There are also always two ciders on offer but these are discretely tucked around the corner of the bar. Douglas sees brewing as a true craft but is rather dismissive of the cider making process and therefore a tad embarrassed when customers praise these over and above his beloved beers.

I gain an early insight into Douglas's approach to beer when we discuss the many festivals popping up across Scotland, some of which are provided as annual events by breweries. "We have beer festivals every day" is his comment and I soon discover that he's not stretching the truth too far. In no time at all he's poured me tasting glasses of all eight beers and both ciders. I sip my way through them but have to engage my resistance, as Brian doesn't drive himself. The bar area presents a homage to beer and is definitely somewhere you could get very comfortable for a long evening of tasting and chat. Of all the bits of kit, memorabilia and general beer-related stuff, I'm taken by both the practical value and alliterative name of the contraption that allows casks to be efficiently drained of their contents into punters' glasses – 'Tilting Stillage'. Douglas is full of ideas for promoting beer in Scotland and clearly has a genuine love for real ale. He's resolutely against using kegs for real ale (a contradiction in terms I know), although I argue that these provide a better stepping stone for new craft beer drinkers to migrate from the fizzy, tasteless super-brands and offer an easier medium for pubs to manage. Before moving on I book a 'brewer for a day' experience and we discuss his plans for a tourist Ale-Trail and how he may promote this through visiting every Scottish brewery with a visitor centre, in one day, in a helicopter. I'd be up for that!

The next day we head to Larbert near Stirling for an appointment with Tryst Brewery. It's quite well hidden and after several tricky three point turns and slow drives up and down the street, the local residents' curtains are beginning to twitch. I therefore park Brian up and venture forth on foot. Still no sign of my prey so I phone the brewer, John, and he executes precise directions by means of waving frantically at me from the end of the road. He's in mid brew and there's another bloke about to shovel the spent barley from the mash tun. I enquire as to whether he uses live or dried yeast in a lame attempt to spark conversation, to which he delivers a short but definitive reply, "real brewers use live yeast". That clears that one up then.

I ask about the name of the brewery and whether it's pronounced Tryst (as in mist) or Tryst (as in diced). "It depends if you're English or Scottish", says John. Tryst as in diced it is then. As you may know, a tryst is essentially a meeting or passing place through which drovers er... drove their cattle. The brewery sits near such an historic zone and hence it's chosen name. You may be familiar with the phrase 'lovers' tryst', being an agreement between lovers to meet at a certain secret place. I like this definition better, especially as lovers may well meet somewhere where they could have a beer. The word actually originates from the old French word triste (as in beast – how many ways can there be to pronounce one word?), being a waiting place for hunters. Confusingly, 'triste' is now the French word for 'sad'. Don't you love etymology? Anyway, I would like to think that the old drovers maybe did do a bit of hunting and drinking on their way to market and quite possibly indulged in the occasional secret meeting with an illicit lover.

On my way back to Edinburgh, where I'll again crash at my son Nick's place, I pop in to see Stuart at the Kinneil Brewery, stowed away at the back of the Corbie Inn in Bo'ness (the brewery, not Stuart). It's my first time in Bo'ness and I'm intrigued to learn that its full name is actually Borrowstounness. This came from when the Burgh of Linlithgow needed a place from which it could ship its goods. The promontory or 'ness' they used for this purpose became known as the 'burgh's town ness', which later mutated into the long version of the name before being mercifully shortened into its present form. Like many small breweries, Stuart uses his copper to double up as a hot liquor tank thus preserving valuable space. He's been a home brewer for many years and, like many of his ilk, has valuable DIY skills used to make, fit and repair the kit. His beers carry old names such as Penn Vael (end of the wall) and Caer Edin (fort on the hill). Brewing brings all manner of challenges, many unforeseen, and Stuart explains how the local water company had recently added chlorination without his knowledge, thereby affecting the head on his beers. I learn, however, that the micro-colander-like thingy on the end of the pub tap helps to add head to the beer and has the lovely name of a 'sparkler'. Sparklers give good head apparently. (I think I just scraped the bottom of the beer humour barrel.)

14 Yeast

"I would kill every last man in this room for one drop of sweet beer"

Homer Simpson

So far, in our journey along the brew kit, we've started with something simple (water), sweetened it up then made it slightly bitter. Clearly a massive over-simplification but it does sound rather like many journeys in life. Having given our grains a bath before boiling the brew with hops, we've now cooled it down in preparation for the next, and perhaps most significant, stage. Ladies and gentlemen, we are going to make alcohol. Can you imagine the joy unconfined when primitive man first accidentally discovered alcohol. Its origins are lost in the mists of time but it's likely that some wild yeast connected with some wet grain or rotting fruit and, not wishing to see it go to waste, some lucky human got a bit merry on the fermented foodstuff. I would suspect that this miracle was the focus of much experimentation over the ensuing years and indeed generations, until a way was found to reliably replicate the process. Once the basics were mastered the human race was on a trajectory that would only gain momentum over the centuries, leading to the intoxicating world that we live in today. Many people shun alcohol of course for personal, health or religious reasons and I completely respect their choices but, for those of us who do imbibe (sensibly, of course), it plays a central role in our social structure, features as a key part of any celebration and is often the catalyst to hours of fun with friends and family, some of which (and whom) we can still recall the next day.

It is then quite remarkable how something so intrinsic to so much of society, is created by something as humble and simple as yeast. I don't know what you picture in your mind when you think of yeast. Maybe it's just a microscopic molecule depicted by letters, numbers and lines on your old chemistry teacher's blackboard? Perhaps it's a cartoon blob with a little face like something from a 1960s educational film? Or perhaps you think of it more like these little squiggly shapes under a microscope, swimming around in a drop of water. Well, all of the above qualify as reasonable estimations of the truth in my book because yeast is in fact a single-celled micro-organism that apparently makes up 1% of the fungus kingdom and reproduces asexually. Basically a mono-cellular, sexually efficient mushroom then! Add it to a sugary substance and it will magically convert those sugars to alcohol under the right conditions. I don't really understand exactly how this works but the best explanation I've heard describes the yeast as absorbing the sugars through its cell walls, causing a chemical reaction that produces heat, CO_2 and, star of the show, alcohol. Of course yeast isn't only used for that purpose. Anyone who enjoys a bit of baking will use a strain of yeast to make the dough rise and give off that lovely, yeasty, fresh-baked bread aroma that we can't resist. It's also the basis, of course, for yeast extract or, more familiarly, Marmite or Vegemite if you're from down under. Here the yeast suspension has salt added that causes it to self-destruct (such cruelty) before being heated up to create the spread that is loved by some as much as it is hated by others.

Back to the brewing process, once the hop wort has been cooled and transferred into the waiting fermentation vats, one of the first things the brewer will do is take the specific gravity measure. This is done once before adding the yeast (original gravity) and again at the end of the fermentation (final gravity). These measures are taken by a hydrometer, which looks a bit like a big thermometer, but wider at one end within which is a weight. The thinner end is calibrated to display the gravity of the liquid it's immersed into, with a reading of 1000 for water. One of the consequences of turning sugar to alcohol is that the liquid becomes less viscous and therefore has less gravity. By measuring the difference between the readings at the start and finish, and applying a cunning formula, the brewer can calculate the alcohol by volume (ABV) that will be indicated on your bottle and recorded for the purposes of calculating duties due to Her Majesty's mates at Custom and Excise. These rates of duty vary depending on the size of your brewery and the alcohol level of your beer. Between 2.8% and 7.5% it's a linear scale but should you venture either side of those boundaries, the tab is suitably adjusted. Brewers are of course very well aware of these formulae and will choose and price their beer accordingly. So how much duty would a brewer pay for a pint of 5% alcohol beer, brewed in a small microbrewery (under 5,000 hectolitres a year)? Right now that would work out at around 28p according to my crude calculations. This is half what you'd pay if you brewed over 60,000 hectolitres a year but, as we learned, these rates are all increasing by 2% per annum above the rate of inflation in the face of significant price pressure at point of sale. The beer lobby are, er, lobbying for change but I'm not sure that the Chancellor is a real ale drinker and no doubt has coffers to fill. (Stop Press: the recent Budget removed this escalator prompting great celebrations among brewers who are now all busy organising a piss-up in their respective breweries.)

The yeast that we are poised to add (or pitch) can be dried or fresh, top or bottom cropping and may be on its maiden mission or a veteran of hundreds of similar forays. Brewers who insist on fresh yeast may look down scornfully on those who opt for the convenience of dried yeast, but it probably makes some practical sense for the small player and some would argue that the end product tastes just as good either way. There are certain styles of beer that do demand live yeast to achieve their particular attributes but otherwise there are probably other more significant influences on the final product. That said, just as I would support hop flowers over pellets, it doesn't seem quite the same to make a craft beer, a natural product, from dried yeast. Those who do favour the fresh stuff differ within their creed in terms of how many times the same yeast can be used. Again, I'm not sure how much difference it makes to your pint but there's something quite charming and authentic about nurturing the same batch of yeast over many years, loyally trusting it to do the same excellent job earning its hundredth cap as it did when it first represented its brewery.

So, that brings us to the question of top versus bottom (fermenting) yeasts. These are simply different kinds of yeast, the former more typically used for ales and harvested from the top of the tank while the latter are more typically adopted for lagers and harvested from the bottom. When the beer cools the yeast cease to be active and the fermentation is over. This is a subject, however, that can require a degree in chemistry or microbiology to fully understand what's going on. I was happiest with the explanation given by one brewer that when the beer is cooled, the yeast join hands (flocculate), go to sleep and fall down.

Fermentation can take anything from a couple of days to a couple of weeks to complete, depending on the type of beer and therefore type of yeast. While our favourite micro-organism's main duty is definitely to receive sugar and deliver alcohol, it also helps to impart some flavour on the way. This part of the process is credited with adding tastes ranging from green apples to butterscotch and, unfortunately, sulphur! It also provides some light carbonation as well as producing heat. This heat needs to be offset by some cooling or the magical transformation won't work properly. Therefore the brewer usually has cooling jackets (not 'cool jackets', I haven't yet met a brewer in cool threads) around the vats to maintain the optimum temperatures for efficient fermentation. The beer can now be left to condition before being pasteurised or filtered if it's destined for a keg (or bottle), or poured into casks (or bottles) if it is to be marketed as 'real ale', therefore enjoying a secondary fermentation after it leaves the brewery.

These vessels and methods all bring with them various degrees of shelf life. Casks have the shortest window within which they must be consumed while kegs keep a bit longer. Bottled beers can last for up to a year but bottled real ales seem to have the greatest longevity of all and can survive for many years unopened – a theory that is rarely tested. Just point the bottle away from you when you finally do open it! Every keg typically contains two volumes of carbon dioxide, squashed down under pressure, so that it all fits in there with the beer, ready to be scooshed up a pipe and out of a tap into your glass. This may sound like a lot of gas but there's actually the equivalent of twice that amount in champagne, which explains why it's called 'bubbly'. Real ale is neither filtered or pasteurised, nor carbonated. The remaining yeast, spurred on by the teaspoon of sugar added to the cask to keep them from going hungry, keep the beer alive and help provide a mild, natural carbonation. As with any food however, what you gain in freshness you lose in hardiness and cask ales will require the very best of care on their way to being gently pumped into your drinking vessel for your heartfelt appreciation. So, drink up; after all the trouble taken to create such a perfect product, it's the 'yeast' we can do. (Sorry, but you can't have a beer book without a few dodgy puns.)

15 Out of the Brew

I've spent most of the last two months celebrating my 50th birthday in some form or another but this weekend the actual anniversary arrived. This is a relief for me as I wasn't feeling too good about entering my 6th decade but now it's here I'm cool with it. It's also a relief for my liver of which I had been demanding even greater levels of performance than usual. It was also becoming clear that my friends were getting a little tired of frequently celebrating an event that still hadn't actually happened. "So, when exactly *are* you 50 Robert?" It's my belief that while for ordinary birth 'day' celebrations a day of festivities will suffice, for years divisible by ten it's not unreasonable to revel in your achievement for as many months as possible. I made a reasonable effort for my fortieth, fitting in my first (and last) tattoo, cycling Cuba and having a wild weekend in Dublin with the guys. Having set that watermark, I felt entirely justified in indulging in a few African safaris, spending a day with gorillas in Rwanda, taking Brian to the sunnier parts of Europe, attending two music festivals, a weekend with the guys in Abergavenny (I know, not an obvious choice) and a family weekend in Edinburgh.

It was just after the big day that I attended a 'Foundation in Brewing' course at the Beer Academy in London. Yes, you read that correctly, 'Beer' Academy. If you're looking for an unusual gift for a good mate who loves his (or her) beer you could do worse than buy him a ticket for this gig. I've been on a few courses and seminars in my life but this was the first one that came with a 'health' warning to say that, as you would definitely be consuming a fair amount of beer it would be best not to drive ("or make any serious plans for the evening" it could have continued). There were maybe 16 or so folk sat around the table in a fairly posh old building in Mayfair that day, ready to soak up lots of information about beer and eagerly anticipating the practical sessions in particular. We sniffed hops, chewed on barley, tasted yeast and gained a decent insight into all the key aspects of brewing. The tasting sessions were nothing if not thorough and generous. Had I imbibed to the fullest extent possible without being rude, I would have been struggling to navigate the stairs at the end. Some of the tasting was carried out with various foods to illustrate just how well beer can be matched to grub.

On the subject of food, not only did I get to try lots of very acceptable beers that day, but they also provided us with enough pizza to obviate the need to buy ingredients for dinner on the way home. So, I left a tad tipsy, very full of pizza and stuffed with fabulous facts about beer or, as I called it when asked for a description, "a refreshing beverage that makes people happy"! A few months later, the spring 2013 issue of CAMRA's Beer magazine popped unexpectedly through my letterbox. I leafed through its pages and found an article that had been written all about the very course that I had attended. There, on page 45, the reader is presented with a nicely framed photo of yours truly and one other chap looking up at our glasses of dark beer, scrutinising its colours in the light. A second and less flattering photo of me inspecting and smelling some hops in my hand follows on page 47. The magazine was a pretty good read despite carrying these unpleasant images.

So, it's back to 'work' and the shortest trip to a brewery yet, just walking distance from my bed in Edinburgh. Barney's Brewery is tucked away behind what was the Royal Dick veterinary college and before that was the site of the Summerhall Brewery in the 18th and 19th centuries. Indeed you can still see the location of the well used to draw the water for the beer and part of the boundary wall of the old brewery. These days the college has become a creative hub for the arts with studio and workshop spaces. Barney himself (actually Andrew Barnett) hails from Wolverhampton and sought brewing as a career from an early age, attending the course at Heriot-Watt before working at the historic Fountainbridge Brewery and later starting his own operation using a former brewery plant connected to a bar in Falkirk. The brewing itself now takes place in what was a stable and the original doors remain, allowing maximum ventilation when things get too hot in the 'kitchen'. So there's a bit of history here but also a thriving contemporary arts scene and the whole place really comes alive during August when the world famous Edinburgh Fringe festival bursts into life. If you have yet to experience the planet's biggest and best festival in the beautiful, historical village of Edinburgh then I heartily recommend that you make a date, take a brolly and soak up the cornucopious entertainment.

Barney claims his brewery to be the only microbrewery in

Edinburgh. This is not only strictly true (Caledonian is probably too big and the others are outside the city) but also quite incredible given the levels of demand, especially in the summer. Real ale drinking is frankly not nearly as widespread and popular in Scotland as it is in most parts of England but the exception is Edinburgh. You don't have to walk far to find a pub with a tempting choice of craft beers and the atmosphere, food and surroundings to match. You definitely can't say quite the same about Glasgow for instance. Why is that? Well, you could glibly class Edinburgh as traditional and Glasgow as contemporary. Edinburgh has a significant English population whereas Glasgow is, well, full of Glaswegians. Edinburgh has the Whisky Society while Glasgow has Irn Bru. The national football ground is in Glasgow, whereas Edinburgh boasts the national rugby stadium. Glasgow is also the home of Tennent's, whose lagers are probably seen by many as the antithesis of real ale. Our two biggest cities are 50 miles from each other and a whole world apart but we cherish them both.

I wish Barney well and head for Bridge of Allan near Stirling, where I'll be camped out for a couple of nights. Actually, I won't be camping at all; I'll be warm and comfortable in a local hotel. It's late November in Scotland so at one level this is an entirely sensible and practical decision given that temperatures regularly fall below zero. I am nonetheless feeling an edge of guilt about not roughing it and a slight loss of camaraderie with poor Brian who will be fully subjected to the elements in the hotel car park. I did look into booking a pitch in the local campsite but to my shameful relief it closes from November for the winter. Phew! Stirlingshire lies at the heart of Scotland and as well as having a significant brewing history, was also the scene of many a famous battle. Stirling's castle sits proudly atop a hill near the town, bearing a strong resemblance to its more famous counterpart in Edinburgh and nearby is the home of the Wallace Monument, remembering the life and near-achievements of our favourite son, William Wallace. I would recommend a visit here to soak up the history, admire his enormous claymore (calm yourselves ladies) and completely erase the image of Mel Gibson from your mind!

After a quiet evening and a peaceful night I grab my wellies from Brian and make my way toward the Tin Pot brewery where I will today pop my brewing cherry by making my own beer. I've no idea how I should have prepared for this but, just in case, I've been thinking about the recipe that I would wish to create. I'd be happy to just make a hoppy IPA but quite fancy creating a beer that has an orangey nose and chocolaty after taste. This was inspired by my childhood craving for Terry's Chocolate Orange. I still can't resist guiltily dropping one in my shopping basket, especially if it's on an impossible to resist offer. I like them chilled so that the chocolate has a bite and the pieces separate easily. The first bite of a segment is always the thin end of the wedge with a couple more bites to finish off the remaining crescent. The pinnacle of any TCO eating experience however is the core. The little crenulated column of chocolate that exists only to anchor the segments but offers a secret bonus once all of these have gone. My lust for this morsel is no doubt fuelled by my mum's insistence throughout my childhood that she always got the core. A salutary lesson for parents everywhere.

My mental preparation comes to nothing however when I discover soon after arrival that Douglas has already chosen the brew for the day and indeed had already stopped by very early that morning to set up the various grains ready to tumble into the mash tun. Importantly, he'd also put the water on to heat up in the copper, where we shall later boil the wort with other magic ingredients. The beer we're making today is Nut Brown Ale. I ponder my response to this news with a slight feeling of loss from my utter lack of creative input but tempered with relief that we're not making something that might arise from the creative mind of an over-enthusiastic home brewer such as banana and passion fruit ale or cinnamon spice bitter. Nut Brown Ale carries a feeling of tradition, sounds like a winter beer, seems to fall within the typical core range of ales and reminds me of my parents' favourite sherry, Walnut Brown. Hopefully it won't taste anything like that though. I don't think we'll be designing a special label for this beer but if we did then I think I'd opt for having a squirrel, a red squirrel in fact, with an acorn between its hands, having a nibble with some autumn brown leaves scattered around and a farming scene in the background, maybe showing the barley being harvested.

I am awoken from my meandering thoughts by Douglas calling me to attention by the side of the mash tun where the water is flowing in and the grains are beginning to drop from above. We have a mix of pale barley malt, dark malt, oats and wheat, the latter helping with head retention as well as imparting some flavour. My job is to stir this all around like a giant bowl of porridge to distribute the grains and avoid any lumps forming. No one likes lumpy porridge. This gets increasingly difficult as the amount of grain increases and the viscosity nears its optimum level. I'm handicapped by skinny arms (mine) and a fear of splashing the contents over the edge, so my performance is average at best. Douglas takes over and when we're done I can only spot one lump, which is despatched into its component parts with a swift swipe of the oar-like implement with which we have been stirring the cauldron.

We leave the brew to infuse the sugars from the grains and retire to the pub area for a coffee and a chat. Douglas shows me the full details of the recipe sheet and I notice that there are three different ingredients included for the purposes of fining the beer. These are necessary, he tells me, for creating a beer that is clear not cloudy as the modern drinker "drinks with his eyes" and generally won't appreciate any lack of clarity in the pint glass. Indeed, Douglas continues, it was the invention of glass that first led to the preference for a clear beer with a frothy head as until then the drinking vessels were made of opaque substances such as pewter so that the drinker couldn't see what he was drinking. (With a glass vessel this effect can still happen but usually after a long session when everything starts to look a bit cloudy.)

The three substances are all of natural origin and do no harm to the quality or flavour of the beer. It still feels a bit strange however to add a silicon based adjunct, copper finings made from Irish moss and finally isinglass, which actually gets added to the cask with the beer. It is this final fining that seems the most bizarre and which also means that strict vegetarians cannot drink most cask ales. Isinglass, as we know, is made from the swim bladders of sturgeon and is produced as a milky concentrate that is diluted for purpose and added to the beer. It certainly does the job of making the beer clear as it pulls all the bits and pieces to the bottom that would otherwise form a cloudy suspension. I do wonder though, given a clear (sorry) choice between a tasty, natural, cloudy beer or a tasty, clear beer that has had liquidised fish innards added, whether tastes may change and opaque drinking vessels may make a comeback! At least it's made from swim bladders and not any other kind of bladder.

We're ready to transfer the wort to the kettle and we're soon operating in a blur of synchronised efficiency. Douglas is transferring the wort bucket by bucket while I get to sparge so that we increase our yield from the barley. The sparging mechanism is a partially automated, semi-integrated, low energy system that essentially involves me pouring hot water through a colander and moving it in a circular motion above the partially spent grains. Like having a shower after a bath. The kettle is soon full and we can add the hops and about half a tub of treacle that shall no doubt impart colour, flavour, sweetness and calories. I absolutely adored treacle as a child (thick, black and molassy and not to be confused with syrup, which is golden and sweet in a sugary sort of way), so I think I'm going to like this concoction. That's good because I'll be taking away a 10-litre supply once it's all fermented and semi-conditioned.

My next job is to clean out the mash tun by scooping the spent grains into sacks that will be taken to a local farm as cattle fodder. These provide good nourishment but unfortunately carry absolutely no alcohol content. I wonder if we added a little yeast whether we might achieve some bovine inebriation and, consequently, a mildly alcoholic milk for our tea and cereal in the morning. Happy cows, happy people. Once the grains are removed we clean and sterilise the mash tun ready for the next brew. While the kettle boils we take a short drive to deliver the alcohol-free barley to the farmer. He's not around and luckily neither is the large and aggressive cockerel that Douglas told me had virtually savaged him one time. We are admiring the excellent condition of the hens when we hear a loud noise that heralds the imminent arrival of his cockiness and within moments we've leapt back in the car and are speeding back to the brewery as the sound of laughing chickens fades into the distance.

We return in time to chuck in the aroma hops before transferring the brew to the fermentation vats to be cooled ahead of the live yeast being later added. The hops in the kettle act as a natural filter, retaining the undesirable solids known, rather onomatopoeically as the 'trub'. We take the chance to nip out for a pleasant lunch, and then on returning to base we commence the tasting. I have 5 examples of Scottish bottled beers in front of me and I'm rather afraid that I might be expected to neck the lot as no one else is partaking. I work my way through about a third of each bottle before being invited to once again make my way through the eight cask beers on tap and both ciders. Craig, the loyal barman, starts filling half-pint glasses but as I would quite like to make it back to the hotel without the aid of a stretcher, I request tasting glasses instead. There are all manner of flavours in these beers and to my palette some work and some don't, but that's as intended as tastes do vary between drinkers. The Gold Pot is the winner for me and, losing the ability to make sound decisions, I decide to try the ciders. I actually quite like these but knowing Douglas's view that cider is wholly inferior to beer and there just for emergencies, I keep quiet. I am now experiencing a heightened feeling of bonhomie and fail to offer any resistance whatsoever to the invitation to have a couple of pints. The conversation was no doubt lively and informative but I remember little of it. Getting drunk in an empty bar with an entirely sober publican is a strange experience. Luckily it was soon time for me to leave and I wobbled back to the hotel enveloped by a fuzzy beer haze. It was no surprise that I crashed out unconscious on the bed but of considerable note that I managed to venture out later for food and a large glass of wine.

The next morning I was feeling decidedly seedy with a nasty combination of hangover and flu. After checking out as late as possible I sat in Brian debating whether to head home or brave at least one brewery visit. Either way I was going to spend the next hour driving and this was probably my last chance to go and see the splendidly named Luckie Ales, so I headed for Auchtermuchty where I recalled they were based. Auchtermuchty is such a quintessentially Scottish sounding place name that on first hearing it you would know immediately which country it belonged to. Those applying to be UK citizens and wishing to settle in Scotland should probably be required to make a faultless, spittle-free pronunciation before being accepted. The town square should have a plaque celebrating its status as the most Scottish sounding town in Scotland. It should be twinned with towns sharing the equivalent accolade in their countries, like Moenchengladbach in Germany or Wagga Wagga in Australia.

I'm trying to think of other suitable twin towns for my destination as we drive along, while congratulating myself on a steady recovery that belies my age. The actual location of the brewery is outside town and it takes me a few drive pasts before spotting the buildings down a bumpy, muddy farm path. Unit number 8 is looking tremendously closed and a local confirms that the brewery that was once there moved away a couple of years ago, but they don't know exactly where. My Internet search uncovers no further clues so I call Mr McLuckie, after whom his beers are named. "I sent you the address in my email" he advises with just a hint of well-deserved scorn. I feel a slight prickle of stupidity as my schoolboy error hits home. My fragile state that morning had fogged my memory and blunted my normally razor sharp preparations and so now, already quite late, I have to drive to Markinch and bid farewell to Auchtermuchty.

My visit to Luckie Ales at the back of a modern industrial park passes without any further diversions and Stuart shows me around the one-barrel capacity brewery that he has put together to produce traditional ales to historic recipes for discerning buyers. Quality over quantity and a predilection for exceptional beers seem to be his trademark. He kindly sends me off with a bottle of his finest that he passes to me with the care one would normally afford to a precious antique. I make my way back to Brian looking forward to the journey home, but decide to first arrange my visit to Stewart Brewery for the next day. I'm obviously not quite back to post-inebriation parity as when the phone is answered I apologise for calling "out of the brew" instead of out of the blue. Freud might have had something to say about that.

I failed to make any further appointments so I pass an easy day, punctuated only by a very pleasant but brief visit to Stewart's just south of Edinburgh. I'm intrigued to learn that they have vessels in the production line that started life either in the dairy industry or in the Irn Bru factory. While maturing beer in whisky casks has the positive benefit of impairing some of those flavours, I'm relieved to learn that no such transference of Irn Bru essence takes place. That would not be a great combination. A common drink in Scotland is lager top where a small amount of lemonade is added to a pint of beer. I have no evidence to suggest that the lemonade is substituted for Irn Bru in parts of Glasgow but someone must have tried it. I'm pretty certain they add it to their whisky at least. And why isn't there an Irn Bru alcopop – surely a winner among those raised on Scotland's 'other national drink'?

It was going to be a long afternoon

at the Tin Pot brewery

16 The Borders

I'm feeling a great sense of purpose as the train speeds me swiftly north toward Scotland's capital city. After 8 weeks of touring Scotland I've had to accept through harsh experience that trying to visit every single brewery is like chasing the end of the rainbow. I have already had to pass on a couple where it was just a bad time to visit, as they were moving to new premises. At least one or two I couldn't find as they were tucked away out of sight and weren't clearly signposted or had no contact details. In addition to these challenges, new breweries have recently opened in Forres and Lossiemouth (and no doubt elsewhere), thus swelling my hit list. I've also decided to pass on cuckoo brewers and anywhere not presently in production such as Fyfe. I live with these imperfections knowing that on any journey you can miss more by trying too hard to find all that you're looking for – deep huh? Nonetheless, I do feel a sense of loss when I know there's a brewery out there that I haven't been able to visit, leaving me with a longing to one day return and scratch that itch.

My sense of purpose then, comes from a desire to achieve my goal this week of visiting all four breweries in the area broadly defined as the Scottish Borders. It's a modest target but it's a matter of pride. So far I have one open invitation and one specific appointment with no response from the other two. I ponder over why it may be that

Scotland has an area specifically named after the border with our southern neighbour while the same isn't true of England. Perhaps it may be intended as a somewhat parochial warning to those travelling south that they have now entered the 'border' area (confusingly referred to as the 'Borders', plural) and are approaching the end of their country. A bit like that voice that chimes out a polite warning that you are reaching the end of the moving walkway. The border itself is 96 miles long and is our only land border (maybe another reason for the unique naming of the region next to it). There was once a disputed area of the border, which led to Berwickshire (and North Berwick) being in Scotland but Berwick upon Tweed in England. This quirk still manifests itself today with Berwick Rangers playing in the Scottish football league, not the English. Hadrian's wall, by the way, does not follow the borderline but in fact lies entirely within England. There was no way those Romans were taking any chances with the heathen Scots!

I'm still two appointments short of my target as I point Brian south toward Jedburgh, guided by Homer's dulcet tones. With some detailed directions and progressing at snail's pace down a pot-holed farm road, we arrive at the Scottish Borders Brewery on the Chesters estate. As I exit Brian I hear a low grunting sound that appears, incongruously, to be emanating from two long-eared, black-faced sheep. I'm relieved to see that the fence between them and me (and Brian) is in good fettle as their sinister stares are becoming somewhat unsettling. I creep round to the brewery, carefully skating over the icy earth, while admiring the rolling fields and snow-capped hills in the distance.

This brewery boasts the slogan 'From Plough to Pint' as they grow their own barley on site as well as brewing the beer. They actually mowed out the image of a giant pint across their fields to produce a striking image to illustrate the grain/beer connection, winning them a prize for their creative marketing approach. Indeed the water supply also comes from an Artesian spring situated on the farm, thus enhancing the homegrown brand. The brewery is less than two years old and initially kicked off by wisely inviting local publicans along to share their views of the beers they wanted to sell and their customers wanted to drink. The range is kept to a few core beers and the alcohol levels don't typically exceed 4.5% - what they call in the business, 'session' beers. Indeed, as I'm chatting to Peter, who's brewing today, a couple of publicans exit with John the owner, having been round to find out more about how to look after cask beers that they may buy from the brewery.

I soon head back to Brian, sneaking past the grunting sheep before gently guiding him up the slippery, bumpy access road. I've asked Homer to take us to Kelso, just ten miles down the road and home to the Tempest Brewery. I haven't got an appointment but it's got to be worth a try while I'm in the 'hood. My timing is good as Gavin is brewing but he's pretty busy so I leave him to it and go to grab some lunch. I soon come across the Border Meringues café at whose sister outlet I had earlier enjoyed a fine coffee. The style is a little traditional and a touch twee but gives the impression of purveying quality 'fayre'. I order the French onion soup, which is indeed very pleasant but comes not with a crouton of French bread and Gruyere on the top as you might expect, but instead with a very Scottish cheese scone on the side. Fusion cooking is alive and well in Kelso.

I stroll back to Tempest who promise 'bigger' beers in their marketing and indeed the range of flavours and alcohol content of their products delivers on this promise. Their approach in many ways complements the simpler range offered by the chaps at Borders. Gavin tells me about a beer brewed in collaboration with Cromarty, made with industrial quantities of pumpkins and aimed at the Halloween market. Every pint is made with about 100g of these edible lanterns I'm told. We're having an amiable enough chat but I've learned to gauge the degree of welcome I'm being afforded as being in direct proportion to how far inside the brewery I get. I'm still standing by the door so it looks like this may be a short visit. Another sure sign is how much the brewer just reacts to questions without offering some unsolicited insights. When this happens I usually last no longer than five minutes. This isn't a criticism of any brewer as I'm genuinely grateful for any time and insights they can offer, but I've learned to read the signs and truncate my visits accordingly. Just as I'm pondering how to bring this chat to a close, Gavin's lunch arrives and it's time to take Brian back up the road before darkness descends. The drive home takes us twisting and dipping through the snow-covered, undulating Borders landscape but our view is partly obscured by the sleet starting to blow into Brian's face. This at least starts to remove the layer of mucky gunge that coated his body after the drive down. I imagine that he's already looking forward to his well-earned winter hibernation.

I'm in positive mood and fine fettle the next day as I've secured an early appointment with Broughton ales, thus achieving this week's goal of seeing all four Borders' breweries. Homer gets us to the village of the same name but then guides us down a narrow, snowy road which seems to be experiencing its own rush hour as hassled parents in capacious vehicles drop their sleepy kids off for another dreary day at school. Brian's not too good with enclosed spaces or noisy kids so I quickly back him out and ease him down another rutted, icy road to where the brewery is located. It's especially cold today so Brian's wipers are stiff with ice and his screen wash has frozen solid. I'm early so I top up his screen wash concentrate, anti-freeze and oil and leave him to thaw a little in the car park.

I'm welcomed inside by Ian and offered a warming cup of tea by the lady on reception. This is one of the older breweries in Scotland, founded by David Younger in 1979, and is steeped in tradition. Ian has worked here for 32 years and clearly knows his way around every nook, cranny, lever and switch of the brew kit. The hot liquor tank is a horizontal affair (I guess most affairs are horizontally oriented) and resembles the tanks you get on the back of lorries carrying fuel, milk or whatever.

The beers here carry names and images that speak of their traditional roots and indicate the target market of the brewery. Here they also make Greenmantle Ale, which I can remember as one of the most prominent ales of my Edinburgh years, although I eschewed this for the range of trendy bottled beers then available. These were a marked improvement on the likes of Tennent's lager (replete with pictures of middle-aged ladies whom I assumed to be barmaids) that I had previously been limited to. Actually, I imagine these ladies only appeared middle-aged to my fourteen-year-old eyes. They were probably no more than thirty, but dressed to look forty. The practice of having images of ladies on these cans actually ran from 1962 to 1991 and must be one of the more iconic and recognisable, if dated, marketing programmes ever created. My personal favourite is the 'housewives' choice' series where a recipe was included alongside their picture. So you had such classics as: Amanda (savoury sausages), Cynthia (spaghetti casserole) and Morag (soused fish). Brilliant.

Broughton Ales is a growing business but there was a time when the brewery was in financial trouble and was rescued by Whim Ales of Buxton who remain as the owners today. Ian tells me that they export to countries across the world including, to my surprise, Italy. I just can't connect that hot, wine-loving, Peroni-drinking country with a taste for traditional Scottish ales with names like Merlin, Old Jock, The Ghillie and Black Douglas. Talking about Merlin, one school of thought suggests that he may be buried not too far away, somewhere on Arthur's Seat in Edinburgh. No one really knows how this extinct volcano came by its name but I like the romantic notion that Camelot may have been built in Scotland's capital by King Arthur, not too far from the present site of the castle.

Ian is busy running around doing his brewing thing while

explaining about the beers, the history and his association with Broughton Ales. I'm invited up a couple of pretty steep ladders to view and sniff the fragrant liquids hiding within the myriad vessels dotted around the premises. The brewery seems to me to be the polar opposite of some of the newer 'built for purpose' examples I've seen in places like Cromarty and I wonder if anyone else will be able to operate it when Ian retires! It's soon time for me to go but not before Ian kindly hands me a few beers and I return my empty cup at reception. Brian is still quite frozen and will clearly need some attention if he is to maintain his normal high performance levels, and a bucket of hot water if I am to have any hope of seeing through his windscreen. Unperturbed I head for Innerliethen where I shall kick my heels for several hours before heading to my final borders destination at Traquair Brewery.

As my appointed time nears, we take the road around the grounds of Traquair House, the oldest inhabited house in Scotland, and take a right turn through an entrance near to the Bear Gates, picking our way gingerly over the slippy, crunchy, icy surface. The Bear Gates don't offer a means of entry as they were last closed in 1745 when the Jacobite army marched south to England. Legend decrees that they shall not again be opened until a Stuart king sits on the Scottish throne. That may be some time. I swing Brian into a parking space by the office and feel him slide gently sideways on the ice before coming to a precarious halt. The afternoon light is presenting the house in all its traditional beauty and it takes me ten full minutes to cover the few hundred metres on foot as I stop frequently to admire the scene and breathe the cool, fresh air. I've been guided to the outside of the west wing where I hope to find the brewery and the brewer, Ian Cameron.

Ian has no sooner greeted me than he is explaining how his assistant has gone off sick and taken some of the key keys with him, therefore probably truncating our tour. The good news is though that we can still access the site of the original brewery and the brewing kit that served former lairds back in the 18th Century and beyond. The brewery had fallen into disuse until 1965 when it was restored and became the first domestic brewery in the UK for many years to hold a commercial brewing licence. As we step inside Ian draws my attention to what appears to be a permanently affixed draught excluder on the door but its purpose, he explains, is not the exclusion of the cold breeze but rather of squirrels (in the summer) and robins (in the winter). I'm not sure why the squirrels wouldn't also want to be in here during our coldest season, but apparently they're too busy collecting provisions for their winter larder.

The hot liquor tank, which doubled as the copper, is in great condition and resembles a grand mediaeval furnace, with the liquid being heated from below by a wood fire. To cool the liquid on its way to fermentation, there are two shallow pools and a giant perforated ladle with which the brewer would repeatedly scoop the liquid back a step until it had reached the desired temperature. The fermentation vessels are next door and are made from a type of Russian oak that is no longer available, so require careful handling to be able to continue to impart their unique contribution to the flavour of the beer. Traquair is the only UK brewery that still ferments its beer in unlined oak vessels, so although the old brewery ceased to be used 18 years ago, the FVs are still part of the new production line. Ian tells me that before the days of using hops for bitterness, they would instead add bark or, bizarrely, rancid cockerels. I'm quite certain that I heard him correctly but it does seem rather odd to make a cock-a-doodle brew! The water of course comes from a local spring and the small but exquisite range of beers is shipped all over the world, enjoying a significant following in the USA as you may imagine. One of the favourites is Jacobite Ale, which includes ground coriander seeds among its ingredients.

Ian's from Jarrow originally and I'm curious as to what brought him here and when. Turns out that when he was a young lad he completed his apprenticeship as an electrician but couldn't find any work. A friend offered the respite of a wee trip to Edinburgh where he bumped into an old school mate who was now married and living in Scotland. Attracted by stories of available employment and a good quality of life Ian moved up and temporarily moved in with his friends in Innerliethen. By this time the 20th Laird of Traquair was redeveloping the historic brewery and came looking for someone to help with the work. While brewing seemed unconnected with his newly learned trade, Ian accepted the opportunity and nearly forty years later he's still there. Indeed there are many press clippings and photos on the walls that tell some of the story of how the brewery got to where it is today and show off Ian's love of motorcycles.

After a quick look at the new, functioning brewery, it's time for me to leave, as the keys to the shop upstairs are keeping Ian's mate company in his sick bed at home. I'm gingerly skating along the path on the sheet of solid ice when I hear Ian calling, waving and brandishing a set of keys. I slip and slide my way back, going as fast as I can so as not to prolong our reunion, but limited by my desire not to come crashing down to the amusement of the watching squirrels and robins. Ian explains that he's found a set of keys that open a door where there may be keys that open a door that might let us through to the shop. It sounds a touch convoluted but Ian seems confident and after a short wait we're inside the shop with its array of beer, various brewing memorabilia and Traquair House souvenirs. There are also more pictures of a significantly more hirsute Ian and the current Lady of the House, Catherine.

This time we really are done and I begin the long, slow, precarious walk back to Brian who thankfully hasn't slid down the hill. Ian returns to the brewery to await his next callers from HM Customs & Excise, who are today making the pleasant pilgrimage from their office in Edinburgh. The light has dimmed a little and the silence is broken only by the satisfying crunch of ice breaking underfoot. I see a thin-looking robin flitting from branch to branch in fruitless search for some morsel of food, no doubt dreaming of the good old days before the draught (robin/squirrel) excluder was fitted. The squirrels seem gainfully employed hiding away their winter stores in places that you imagine they may struggle to relocate in the bleak months ahead. I ease Brian out of the ice-rink that has been masquerading as his parking spot and manoeuvre him back to the welcoming tarmac of the A72. The light continues to fade during the drive home, throwing changing shades and shadows on to the gently undulating arable land, chilling out under its blanket of frost.

Traquair House

The brewery is reached on the left by the trees

17 Beer

"Give my people plenty of beer, good beer, and cheap beer, and you will have no revolution among them."

Queen Victoria

Beer is the third most popular drink in the world after ale and lager. No, that's clearly not true. It's the third most popular after water and tea. This means that it beats staples like coffee, milk and juice. That seems to me to be a pretty stunning statistic. It also means that beer is the most popular alcoholic drink in the world. It might also be the drink we spend most money on, as it's clearly more expensive than water or tea. Beer must also be one of life's greatest 'reward' drinks. After a hard day at the office or hours spent doing DIY at home, sitting down with a pint in your local pub feels like a well-earned luxury. Having a coffee with a friend one morning or a glass of Sancerre with lunch are both very pleasant pursuits but they don't have that "I'm finished, I'm tired and I need a special reward" feeling. It's alcohol but it's also refreshing and performs very well as a temporary food substitute. Sure you could mix a cocktail if you were sitting outside in the sunshine but after a hard day we usually don't have the time, energy or the weather for that pastime.

Beer also mixes very well with sporting occasions. Whether you're at the hockey game in Chicago or you're shoulder to shoulder with likeminded footie fans in a pub in North London, I'm willing to bet that the drink in your hand will be a beer, nine times out of ten. Travel tends also to multiply my beer intake. It's less to do with just drinking more in general, arising from the freedom of being on holiday, but more because you can usually rely upon better standards of beer than most other alcoholic drinks. Wine, for instance, can be a serious gamble in some places. I once returned a bottle of red in Addis Ababa that was completely corked. The bar manager couldn't understand what was wrong with it and was utterly confused when I explained that I wanted another bottle of the same type. He charged me for both. With beer however, I have yet to visit any country that doesn't have at least one very acceptable brand to add to the ultra-distributed Heineken that seems to appear everywhere. From Cuba to Cambodia, Panama to Portugal and Belarus to Belize it's what we are most likely to drink, wherever we are on this vast planet.

We've so far strolled gently through the beer-making process from the source of the liquor, via the barley and hops to the wonderful alchemy triggered by the yeast. At one level it is an extremely simple process - soak barley, boil with hops and add yeast. At another level there are myriad variations to this magical and mysterious transition that only a degree level chemist and/or brewer of many years experience could get close to fully understanding. Now that we have created this lovely liquid we need to put it somewhere so that it may be transported to where it shall meet its new owner; typically a very brief but happy relationship. Kegs and bottles are fairly ubiquitous and we've probably said enough about them elsewhere in this book. Casks though do have a degree of folklore, mystery and magic to them and deservedly so. We've talked about breweries being a certain number of barrels in size. Barrels are 36 gallons in volume whereas your typical pub cask holds only 9 gallons. This perfectly formed vessel is known as a firkin, from the old Dutch word for one fourth. That's enough information for most people but just because I love the names I'm going to take you a little further. Half a firkin is a polypin, while half a barrel is a kilderkin. Above the barrel we have, in order, a hogshead, puncheon, butt and tun. A tun is a double butt, which itself is a triple barrel. Wouldn't maths at school have been much more interesting if taught this way? "Children, if two barrels are a puncheon and three kilderkins are a hogshead, how many pints does the farmer need to drink before he falls over?"

I have had the art of cask management explained to me several times and I'm afraid that I still couldn't explain it properly to someone else. So, here goes. In essence the cask seems to have two holes, one for breathing and one for extracting liquid. (Humans are much more evolved having at least twice as many orifices for similar purposes.) The liquid extraction bit seems fairly straightforward, especially if it is simply tapped (to manage the flow) and propped up on tilting stillage (to enable the flow). Obviously one needs a pump to help it on its way from cask to glass if the latter is higher than the former, as would be the case in virtually every pub. The breathing hole, in the middle of the curved surface, seems to be one of those things that you require a bit of a knack to manage properly (I'm still talking about casks, not humans). It's basically used to clean and fill the cask before a stopper, called a shive, is hammered in. The live beer is creating CO_2 and some of this gas needs to escape to achieve the right level of carbonisation in the beer. To control this balance the cellar person (they're not all men) hammers in a spile that can allow gases to escape. Once we're at the optimum level of gassiness this spile, which is made of soft wood, is replaced by another made of hard wood, to stop the gas escaping. When the cask is in use the spile is removed to allow air to get in. Balancing the beer/air/CO_2 equation will help sustain the beer through its short lifespan. Just for the record, the bit at the centre of the shive that the spile breaks through is called a tut. While all of these shenanigans are going on on top of the cask, the bit where the beer will come out, the keystone, has had a tap bashed in from whence the nectar will flow. If you can get all of this right, keep your cellar temperature around 11-13C, your pipes and glasses clean, remember to rotate your stock and be ready to turn on the charm and charisma when front of house then you're all but qualified to be a first rate landlord, or lady.

So, now you know all about the multi-faceted process that is required to deliver that well-earned pint you're nursing, how do you feel about the £4 of your hard-earned shekels that you've just parted with to complete the transaction? You can reckon that somewhere close to one of these pounds will have been paid to the brewer from which he needs to meet all of his production costs of which duty may well be the largest followed by labour, plant/premises and transport. The actual ingredients make up a fairly small fraction of the whole thing, probably less than 2% of the price of your pint. The pub owner may at this point appear to be doing rather well out of the whole deal as he's making a gross profit of about £3 per pint. These chappies will however insist that profits are skimpy at best on beer and they make their living from other drinks and especially food. That is of course due to the high fixed costs of running a pub but it does seem like the closer you get to the customer the more mark-ups seem to increase. Also, I can never understand why restaurants, designed to serve food, say they make more profit from drinks while bars, set up to serve drink, say they make more profit from food. Surely it just depends on which sales you set against your fixed costs and which you treat as marginal? Anyway, enough of all this analysis and hand-wringing over where your money goes, who gets it and who's making the bigger buck. Your £4 pays for one thing and one thing only in my humble opinion – a wonderful, life-enhancing, delicious, social experience. Either you think that's good value and you'll be back at the pub next week or you don't and you'll be loading up at the discount supermarket instead. Only if you're really in a bad way should you even consider giving up beer altogether!

18 Hibernation

Brian is waiting patiently for me in his temporary, hired parking space right outside the offices of Pufferfish in Edinburgh's Southside. The week ahead brings us to a milestone of ten weeks together during which we have covered thousands of kilometres (he doesn't do miles) from Islington to Unst, Inverness to Inverary and Thurso to Kelso. I also feel a little sad, as it's now time for Brian's hibernation to begin. The habits of a Scottish winter morning are becoming more prevalent with windows needing scraped of ice, an engine too cold and brittle to turn over when requested and my nervous checking of the weather forecast in fear of stranding us in a snowdrift. These conditions come as no surprise as we approach the winter solstice at 56° north of the equator, saved from Alaskan conditions only by the warmer currents of air carried from the Gulf of Mexico by the prevailing winds. We will be reunited though, just ahead of the Ides of March, to complete our journey across the brewery map of Scotland.

We have three appointments to fulfil today, beginning with the cleverly named Alechemy Brewery near Livingston, west of Edinburgh. James, the owner and brewer, was previously in pharmaceuticals before turning his hand to brewing; 'turning grain into gold' as he puts it. I'm a little early and there's a breakfast shaped hole in my tummy so I go in search of healthy sustenance, but settle instead for a coffee from a machine in a fuel station and a Double Decker chocolate bar. Alechemy looks like it means business. James has researched the market, created a solid business plan and set himself up with a ten-barrel brewery, bringing years of experience as a home brewer as well as being a chemist. As we chat, he and his dad, Adam, are piling grain into a purpose built wooden hopper called a grist case, ready to be dropped into the mash tun and mixed with the soft water from the local reservoir. The waters are so soft around here (as they are across most of Scotland) that salts must be added to improve the mash efficiency, a critical measure of a successful brew.

James does a little bit of brewing for other parties such as a lager that is shipped down to a pub in east London. Making lager takes a little longer due to the lower temperatures required, causing the fermentation by the yeast to slow down. Lager comes from the German word meaning 'to store' as they had to find methods for the brewing process to work in colder temperatures that therefore required longer storage while the sugars turned to alcohol.

We talk about the migration route for traditional lager drinkers into craft beers and I learn that the best selling brand in the UK is an American beer that uses only 50% barley, lots of rice and various chemicals to create a cold, fizzy lager, short on taste but long on shelf life, that will leave you a little worse for wear the next morning. We talk also of the plethora of new breweries opening around Scotland, testing each other's knowledge of these fledgling hopefuls. How many of these will thrive or even survive over the next few years as the market nears its saturation capacity and the retailers stick with their tried and trusted gaggle of suppliers? These competitive conditions may suggest that to consolidate and flourish brewers will have to look at moving upstream to create their own pubs and bars where they can pocket the extra profits, guarantee some demand and diversify into complementary food as well as other types of drink.

As I'm leaving, James kindly fills my arms with three of his bottled beers and Adam adds an Alechemy mug to the pile. Apparently they're awaiting the arrival of Dave from DemonBrew, who I'm seeing tomorrow, to come and do some bottling with assistance from two Heriot-Watt brewing degree students. This is a great example of the brewing community working together to help each other through the shared challenges of a small but growing industry. There are but a few perceived black sheep in the wider brewing family, Adam describing one crew as a 'right bunch of a**eholes', before qualifying his generalisation to a small subset of that particular brew house. Brian and I head off in search of Sauchie on the edge of Alloa (emphasis on the first syllable, I'm told), nestled close to the Ochil ('Oh kill') hills that give their name to Ochilview, the home of Alloa Athletic FC. Our route takes us over the Clackmannanshire Bridge, all new and shiny compared to its neighbour, Kincardine, built in 1936. Oldest of all of course is the Stirling Bridge, famous for the Scottish victory over the English in 1297 at the eponymous battle that took place thereon.

We park up at the Mansefield Arms, home to the Devon Ales

Brewery, housed behind the pub. This is very much a pub and not a bar. It's resolutely aimed at local trade; a workingman's watering hole. The beer made behind the scenes retails at £1.85 a pint at the tap – remarkably cheap at point of sale but almost twice what a brewer would get by selling his casks direct to trade. Hand pulls are not used here (they're 'English not Scottish') so the beer is delivered instead by CO_2 driven pumps. The 70-shilling and stout that I try come with healthy heads, assisted by the sparklers on the taps. These beers are designed to be drunk over an evening and Martin, the landlord, believes that the test of a good beer isn't in the tasting glass but rather in the quality and pleasure of the third pint. He may be right but how many people would still be conscious for their fourth sample? The ingredients of the beers are kept simple and around 20 casks a week are produced, primarily for use here and in the sister pub a few miles up the road.

We're sitting at a table at the back of the small lounge, annexed on the other side of the bar from the principal drinking den in the heart of the pub. Martin's infant daughter sits with us at the table and is silently tuning into our beer chat while demolishing a newly prepared plate of chicken nuggets. We talk about the significant history of brewing in the Alloa area which continues today but once boasted names such as Younger's, Maclay's, Caulder's and Knox's. We take a look at the cramped space that houses the brewing equipment and Martin explains that the former miner who had worked with him here for many years had recently died and a young apprentice was now slowly learning the ropes. The name Devon Ales comes from the name of a colliery that had once existed near the river of the same name before closing along with many of its contemporaries some forty years ago. This village, the pub, the beers, the clientele and the history all give a feeling of tradition and community that sits well with footy on the telly, a Scotch pie and a few pints of heavy. Not a bad night out.

Next, I head directly for Bridge of Allan and the Tin Pot Brewery where my 10 litres of Nut Brown Ale await. I park up and as I'm exiting Brian I see a hunched, shivering figure, wrapped up against the cold, making his way to Douglas's car. It takes me a moment to realise that it is indeed he and I learn that he's been suffering from a particularly nasty lurgy and is heading home to recover. He pauses his retreat long enough however to fetch my 'bag in a box' and let me taste some of our brew from the tap. I can tell from Douglas's expectant grin that he thinks I'm going to like it and it does indeed go down very easily for a 5% dark ale. Somewhat darker than expected actually, more of a nut black stout than a nut brown ale perhaps, but if anyone asks we can always say – it's 'not' brown. I have again failed to secure an appointment with the elusive Williams Brothers, makers of the famous Fraoch Heather Ale, so return home for an early night ahead of the important task that awaits me the next day – hibernating Brian.

The big day arrives and I've already emptied Brian of anything that's better off back home like Homer, my driving CDs and the mini-Brian money box that mum and dad gave me for my 50th. This last item will be used to gather sufficient £2 coins to fund some interior decoration. Next, it's up to the local garage where I park Brian at the jet wash to give him a decent clean, all the while suspecting that he'll get just as manky again before we get to his winter resting place. There's ice all over the jet wash area so my progress around Brian is super cautious. The jet gun (more like a jet shotgun) is unwieldy at the best of times but as I have no purchase on the ground, the force of the water propels me backwards on the ice. I try to correct my stance but only succeed in turning circles instead of stopping. The gun is out of control now and there are pedestrians on the pavement wondering where the sudden 'rain' shower came from. Through a significant effort of strength and balance I eventually regain control and return to my task, grateful for my new found ice skating skills. A much cleaner Brian takes me on our last journey of the year but before I put him to bed we have one more brewery to visit – the 36th of our trip so far.

Dave brews the DemonBrew beers in the Gothenburg microbrewery at the back of the pub of the same name. Dave's busy when I arrive so I chat to a bloke who explains some of the history of brewing in the area and the Gothenburg principles. These principles arose in Gothenburg, Sweden, designed to better manage and limit the consumption of alcohol while benefiting the community. Consequently the principles require that after a dividend of 5%, all other profits are used to promote the arts and improve the local economy. Many communities within Scotland adopted these principles in one or more of their public houses, where they promoted greater abstinence, non-alcoholic drinks or at least taking food with alcohol. The walls of this bar are festooned with wonderful photos from those times and of the old Fowler Brewery, staffed almost entirely by women. Contrast and compare that image with some of the other photos capturing the visit of one of the former Tennent's lager lovelies. Oh how the role of women in the beer industry has changed!

The microbrewery is visible from the main bar and through the window I can see that Dave is now free so I join him in the small, but very clean and tidy, space. (He confesses to being a stickler for cleanliness, which is no bad thing.) Prevention is better than cure so he brews closer to 4, than the maximum 5, barrels so that the froth doesn't escape from the fermentation vats, creating a nasty, sticky mess. Dave's got a background in IT but has also been a home brewer and, like so many, held a wish to give brewing a go on a greater scale. I like the feel of brewing in a space from which we can see the pub and the punters (were it open yet) and they can observe the process that will deliver a couple of taps worth of real ale for their delectation.

I bid farewell to Dave and make the short trip to the caravan storage facility. It's not as short as it should have been though as Homer takes us down another of his favourite farm-track roads which eventually winds to a halt at a dead end with a few crumbly houses around. At this point a fairly crumbly gent emerges from one of the houses carrying a cigarette, a very strong cup of tea (with bag but without milk) and very few teeth. Those that still remain look like very shoogly pegs. I'm very clearly not 'local' and he enquires after my destination. His directions are almost certainly flawless if only I could understand a word he's saying. I think I've got the gist so we retrace our steps and soon we're onsite and parking Brian in the space where he shall slumber until spring. The owner kindly gets me some soapy water and a brush so that I can bath Brian before slipping on his grey onesie pyjamas. Clean, warm and safe, I leave him to slumber knowing that I'm going to miss us being together on our little adventures and spending long, cold, dark nights with only each other, a classic British sitcom and a couple of free-sample ales for company.

19 Keeping it Real?

Does ale have to be real to be really good? If there was one question that I wanted to have answered from visiting all these breweries then this was it. Everyone has heard of CAMRA, the Campaign for Real Ale, and most people probably have at least a vague idea of what real ale actually is and whether they're part of the fraternity that would call themselves real ale drinkers. When CAMRA started out in 1971 they were very much about campaigning, lobbying, popularising and generally making the case for something that was becoming marginalised, shunned and almost forgotten by a new generation of beer drinkers and a new generation of beers. This change in tastes may in part have been caused by the 'stick' of not wishing to follow the preferences of an older generation whose lifestyles probably seemed at best irrelevant to the young people who frequented bars (not pubs) and for whom clubs meant dancing not dominoes and darts. The stick was important but the carrot was critical. Markets were opening up across borders, bringing an influx of attractive, cosmopolitan foreign beers from Europe, America and beyond. It wasn't just about what you were drinking but what you were seen to be drinking. With these new brands came smart advertising campaigns aimed at exactly this emerging market of young people with cash in their pockets and leisure time on their hands. It didn't matter if that cool Czech beer was brewed in middle England as long as the label said about you what the adverts said about the beer: cool, fresh, fun, bubbly and bohemian.

How on earth could the local pub with its fire in the hearth, jolly landlord and traditional grub possibly compete? They may have added a few modern taps or bottles to satisfy the tastes of their fringe customers who happened to pop in or were accompanying a regular, but they knew what their reliable clientele desired. The demographics were working against them as much as the marketing messages were passing them by. The traditional pints, the real ales that were brewed somewhere down the road, delivering warm, flat beer by hand-pulled pump into a mug (not a glass) were being marginalised. I suspect that CAMRA probably did as much to further alienate the modern lager drinking camp and to highlight exactly why they didn't desire real ales as to promote their attributes as intended. They also, however, offered a call to arms, a common message and a place of refuge for the 'ale'ing troops as they retreated into their comfort zone and ridiculed the brash new wave and their desire for tasteless, fizzy, mass-produced, chemical-infused lagers. They stuck to their task and if nothing else offered a lifeboat to the industry to keep it alive and afloat while time passed, tastes changed and the cycle of fickle fashion slowly made its way back around.

So, what exactly is 'real' ale as opposed to ordinary (fake?) ale, craft beer or any other kind of fermented beverage? How do CAMRA define and delineate their target market from everything else? How should that definition evolve to continue to meet their purpose and indeed has that purpose itself evolved from where they started? Is that definition in danger of doing as much harm as good to their cause? Are they promoting the consumption of ale that is real at the expense of ales that may not be 'real' but are definitely really good? I guess I'll need to address what I mean by 'really good' at some point as well, if we are to exit this chapter with more answers than questions.

What's your perception of real ale, reader? I mentioned beards and chunky jumpers earlier on and intentionally evoked the stereotype with mention of words like 'warm' and 'flat' (referring to the beer not the drinker of course). Would you know if the ale you were drinking was 'real' or not and actually would you even care? How do you define a 'really good' pint and what would you be at pains to avoid when making your selection from the range of beers and ales presented in front of you? Have you even given the matter a moment's thought, as maybe you already know what you like and where to get it? Well, I don't think we can progress much further with our journey without delving into how CAMRA define the 'RA' that they have been so long CAMpaigning for.

If you look up CAMRA's website, you will be able to read their definition of real ale. The key statement is as follows: "Real ale is a beer brewed from traditional ingredients (malted barley, hops, water and yeast), matured by secondary fermentation in the container from which it is dispensed, and served without the use of extraneous carbon dioxide." I can identify three key points within this helpful sentence:

1. Traditional ingredients
2. Secondary fermentation
3. No added carbon dioxide

In addition they say: "Brewers use ingredients which are fresh and natural, resulting in a drink which tastes natural and full of flavour. It is literally living as it continues to ferment in the cask in your local pub, developing its flavour as it matures ready to be poured into your glass." So, secondary conditioning (or fermentation) in the container from which it shall be dispensed, as compared to being conditioned only in the brewery seems to be the key difference. The 'fresh and natural' requirement could just as easily apply to many breweries that have absolutely no intention of creating any beers that are still alive when they leave the brewery. Hop pellets, dried yeast, fining agents, flavourings, other grains etc. may all be acceptable, but without it continuing to ferment, it's not real ale. I'm not going to argue with the definition at all as CAMRA clearly have complete authority over that but I am going to explore the definition and see if it's helpful to the greater purpose of promoting delicious beer, or not.

So, 'traditional ingredients' is where we shall start. This could be interpreted as being anything that's been used in beer making during the last couple of centuries or it may be taken to mean just the core ingredients that they list above. If it were the latter then we've probably just lost a significant portion of the real ale market because very many of these will include other grains like wheat or oats and all manner of flavourings. Do they really mean to exclude any ale that includes one or more adjuncts? If we interpret their meaning more generously then those beers I just wiped off the real ale map may be reinstated without further questioning, but we may wish to draw the line at rancid cockerels and tree bark. My understanding from the brewers I met is that as long as the ingredients are 'fresh and natural' then CAMRA are usually quite content. Where there did seem to be some furrowing of brows was in the matter of hop pellets being used instead of hop flowers. Hop pellets may be natural but they're certainly not fresh. One could make similar arguments with fresh (clue's in the name) or dried yeast. As far as I could tell however, CAMRA brows were slowly un-furrowed and approval was generally gained as long as the beer was last seen alive leaving the brewery.

Jumping to the third requirement for a moment, I think the artificial carbonisation thing is pretty clear-cut. Either your beer gains some natural effervescence from the secondary fermentation or you have to create the fizz by adding gas under pressure. So, this third point essentially seems to be very closely related to the second one. The crux of this argument then seems to come down to the effect of secondary fermentation on the quality and flavour of the beer. Other than some arguments about which ingredients pass the CAMRA litmus test and which don't, it would appear that real ale is defined by the presence of live yeast, doing their thing, in a bottle or cask, right up to when you drink it.

So, why is secondary fermentation such an important matter? Is it simply a matter of tradition or perhaps to ensure absolute differentiation from the mass-produced lagers? There's no doubt that real ales offer a particular texture due the natural carbonization, but this can lead to a lack of head and a weak 'soupiness' if they aren't expertly cared for. The thing is that there are a great many fabulous beers that satisfy most of CAMRA's requirements but not this one, thus excluding them from the party. I would generally refer to these as 'craft' beers and would offer a broad definition to be: "Craft beers are brewed primarily from water, barley, hops and yeast and they have no artificial additives. Brewers only use ingredients that are fresh and natural, resulting in a drink that tastes genuine and full of flavour. These beers may come in bottle, keg or cask and are typically produced in small quantities." I could have missed out that last sentence but I wanted to explicitly include real ales as a subset of craft beers. Perhaps someone needs to start the CAMCraB (Campaign for Craft Beer) and one day there shall be a merger between that body and CAMRA and we can all live happily (or hoppily) ever after!

I said that I would try to define 'really good' so that we would have something to compare with 'real'. This is of course quite impossible as we're dealing with the wonderful world of human tastes and preferences, which by their nature are beyond definition. One man's Carling is another man's Nut Brown Ale and all that. I know people who live off frozen and processed food, takeaways and McDonald's. To them, this is what they define as food and, yes, they think it's really good. I'm pretty close to the other end of the scale and other than occasionally ordering a pizza delivery I would avoid all of the above like the plague. Remember my friend Greg's revelation about demanding the same standards from his beer as his food – natural and additive free? So in carving out a definition for 'really good', I will be drawing on the beer equivalent of what nutritionists, foodies and health-oriented folk would consider 'really good' to eat. Cold, fizzy, mass-produced lager with limited flavour might be exactly what you like and pretty much everyone will fancy one at some point, but while these can be really good sometimes, they are not craft beers.

My definition of 'really good' is exactly how I've defined craft beer above and therefore in my humble opinion *ale does not have to be real to be really good*, but we are delighted to have the secondary fermentation chappies proudly in our midst. If you yearn for that yeasty, less fizzy, totally 'real' experience and nothing else will do then that's absolutely fine. Some may go further and shun the use of finings, embracing the translucent over the transparent. Others may insist on having only those four core ingredients in any beer they consume. I want my beer like I want my food – fresh, natural, tasty and with lots of variety. I'm happy to eat organic food and I'm happy to drink real ale but neither is at all necessary to meet my criteria for being really good. I feel so much better now that I've got that off my chest.

I don't want to leave this chapter without taking some time to appreciate the importance of beer management in the pub and particularly in the cellar. Ales that are not real, be they craft or not, complete their conditioning in the brewery. To make them palatable for the public they may be pasteurized, filtered or both. Filtration is exactly as you would imagine and can be done to differing degrees known as rough, fine and sterile. The last of these will pretty much remove everything including some colour and body. If you see water coming out the other side then you've gone much too far on the filter spectrum! Pasteurising beer has pretty much the same principles and purposes as pasteurizing milk or any other substance. Some drinkers reckon that this process slightly affects the quality of the beer, giving it a 'cooked' flavour. This may well be true as the beer is heated up to 60C in order to kill any bacteria that may have found their way into our brew. Real ale of course uses neither of these processes and the beer remains a living product with the yeast 'feeding' on the wee bit of sugar with which the bottle or cask is primed.

I've already covered the exemplary skills that the landlord requires to ensure perfect delivery of excellent real ale and I know from personal experience the difference it makes. I have tried the same ale in different pubs and left with quite disparate impressions. This has led me to seek out pubs that know what they're doing and if I'm in any doubt at all I always ask to try one or two before purchasing. There really isn't anything quite like well-crafted real ale, expertly managed and freshly delivered. That's why pubs used to employ dedicated cellar men. The flipside to this is of course that consistency in the quality from pub to pub is not something you can rely on and another reason to seriously consider a craft beer as a viable alternative. So, know what you like and what you're looking for from your beers;

enjoy real ale at its best but tread carefully in pubs you don't know and, wherever you are, try the local craft beers, however they've been conditioned, bottled, kegged or casked. If you think that it's really good, then it's really good. Really.

20 Reunited

I can remember clearly, that cold day in December, when I left Brian to sleep through the harsh winter ahead, thinking how pleasant it would be to come along on a sunny spring day in March to dust him down, pick him up and ride off together to the sound of birdsong and the sight of cherry blossom trees in new bloom, their pink flowers swaying gently in the slight breeze. You can imagine then how my heart sank when I checked out the forecast to find that sub-zero temperatures and snow were expected to forge an unwelcome habitat for our happy reunion. I did think about postponing but appointments had been made, travel had been booked and, at the end of the day, you just have to get on with it. That is of course fine for me to say but I was giving little thought to the shock that poor Brian would feel when he awoke to discover that, far from the warm touch of spring sunshine he was expecting to enjoy, the weather was now actually worse than when he started his hibernation. If he could speak then I'm sure he would have remonstrated at length with me about my timing and my inconsideration, and protested loudly about having to perform in such extreme conditions.

I made my way to Edinburgh by train, connecting with the local service to Prestonpans where the owner of the campervan storage facility picked me up and took me to be reunited with Brian. He had already, very kindly, removed Brian's cold, wet onesie and taken it inside to dry off a bit, having shaken off the worst of the icicles. I checked Brian over and there was but one obvious new flaw that had developed during my absence – his aerial had snapped off. This was most likely due to the weight of the cover bearing down and being pulled by the wind but it may just have frozen to a crisp! Whilst a loss of sorts, it was far from a serious injury given that we could never get decent reception anyway and the aerial could be moved neither up nor down. It did mean however that a new aerial set would have to be added to the Brian shopping list. Otherwise he was looking much as I had left him and the dehumidifying agent had done a fine job of pulling about two pints of moisture from within Brian's body and safely depositing it in the waiting tray. I could therefore delay no longer the real acid test of his roadworthiness – would he actually start up?

My first turn of the key produced a horrible low grunt that sounded like I'd drained the last tiny pulse of power that remained in the depths of his frozen battery and used it to achieve a single turn of the engine. The next couple of attempts produced only silence and I was preparing mentally to find a Samaritan with jump leads. Stoically I persevered and the next few attempts again produced some noise that may have been distantly related to an engine starting but were still quite unsettling. I decided to risk a little more choke and, in a Norman Wisdom moment, it virtually came away in my hand with about eight inches of cable attached. This did concern me a bit as it had never moved more than an inch before without getting stuck. Choke safely replaced I persevered and the noises were becoming ever more awful but their volume and length were heading in the right direction. Somewhere around the fourteenth turn of the key he burst into life, coughing, spluttering and sounding rough as hell but he was alive! I slipped his fresh new tax disc into its holder, adjusted the mirrors and plugged in Homer before gently guiding Brian out onto the road, like we'd never been apart.

I had set myself a target of seeing six breweries over the following two days. It could have been seven but the smallest, Madcap, were unable to entertain me as the owner was off on a couple of weeks' holiday. Having stayed the night with my son, Nick, in Edinburgh, I was awake bright and early the next morning to load up Brian and spark him into life. There had been no more snow, it was cold but with only a few clouds in the sky; the weather seemed to be smiling upon us as we kicked off the last phase of our brewery expedition. With 36 successful visits already behind us, I had set an ambitious revised target of reaching a total of 60 by the end of April. We crawled through Edinburgh's rush hour traffic, eventually escaping onto the M8 toward Glasgow, a route that I used to ply daily when I lived up here. Massive road works and a significant accident seriously slowed our progress and I shuddered to think how I could have suffered this every day at peak times for years on end. Our first appointment of 2013 was with Strathaven (pronounced Strayven) Ales near the town of the same name. It's a bit out of the way and each time we turned off one road, following Homer's instructions, we found the next one to be narrower, more twisty and with a thicker covering of ice and snow. Soon though I was guiding Brian gingerly down the icy approach road to the brewery where I was greeted by two blokes and several dogs.

The brewery is beautifully set on the banks of the Avon River and the surrounding countryside was looking resplendent in its white winter jacket. I parked Brian at the edge of a small snowdrift and padded back to meet with Craig at reception. After jolly hellos and a fine cup of coffee I was passed on to Peter, another of the Heriot-Watt alumni, to show me around. The first thing that strikes you in the brewery is the circular stone wall cladding wrapped around the kettle. This was created in 1993, when Williams Brothers first owned the brewery, before they moved on to their larger premises in Alloa. The mash tun is full of grain and water that shall eventually emerge as Claverhouse, a red ale named for John Graham of Claverhouse, better known as Bonnie Dundee. We complete our tour around the brewery and I notice that I'm tending to do more of the talking these days; to be expected I guess but a habit I shall try to overcome.

I thank Peter and repair to the office for a wee chat with Craig about the industry, which he feels is becoming saturated with too many microbreweries these days. My knowledge of beer and the industry is still relatively nascent but I've soaked up enough knowledge (and beer) to just about hold my own with the professionals. Craig furnishes me with a bottle of '500', created to celebrate their 500th brew, as I make my exit and slither back to Brian. I ease him away from the thick snow and carefully point his nose at the small ski slope masquerading as my exit ramp; but as I try to gain momentum, another vehicle makes its entrance. Etiquette demands that I give way so we're back at the bottom, momentum stifled.

Several attempts to gain traction fail to get us anywhere so I reverse Brian up to a piece of solid ground, rev his engine and shoot up the hill, while trying to keep his meandering back end in line with the front.

Homer's memory banks are well out of date and this motorway we're now on is clearly new, so before long he is babbling absolute nonsense while his screen shows that we are traversing some kind of urban desert. I guide him onto some older roads and before long he's picked up the scent again and we're off to WEST Brewery, nestled next to Glasgow Green. The impressive building that now houses the brewery, bar and restaurant, used to be the Templeton Carpet Factory, which was originally modelled on Doge's Palace in Venice. It's a lovely building in a very pleasant setting and here at WEST they are committed to following the ancient German quality standard, known as the Reinheitsgebot. This means that they are limited in terms of the ingredients they can use and the styles they adopt. All of their beers are kegged bar one line that is bottled. These are all very much craft beers, not real ales, and I must admit I am drawn to the ideals of limited ingredients, modern process and creative products. The beer here has bubbles added and it's served cold but the similarities to mass-produced lagers ends there.

They create quite a range of beers from lager to wheat and even stout. Douglas, who is showing me around, tells me he graduated in maths before deciding to let the brewer in his heart lead the accountant in his head. He pours me some of the maturing wheat beer, called

Hefeweizer, which is being stored at -2°C. It's pretty tasty considering it's still days from being ready. I have a half pint of the real thing later over lunch and it is indeed quite delicious (lunch was pretty nice too). They use a mash filter here, which I have never seen before. It looks like a rack of the trays beekeepers use, hanging down, with gauze across them to capture the unwanted solids. The whole brewing process is controlled through a computer that has what looks like the most complicated flow diagram ever, showing on the screen. This is an ambitious business with a strong vision and I'm not surprised to hear that they are gearing up for expansion to a new brewing site at Port Dundas next year. Luke, the head brewer joins me for a chat over lunch. He's from Maine but spent 6 years in Germany where he grew to love their beer culture. We talk about the American craft beer movement and how 'real ale' doesn't typically feature there. I really do believe that craft beers should be an ally for real ale, not a foe, as they both hold to so many similar principles and a large proportion of drinkers may migrate between the two styles.

I clamber back aboard Brian and we program Homer for my B&B in Annan. I have one more appointment today but I'll be seeing Andrew's Ales a bit later on as the eponymous brewer has a day job to attend to. It's another pretty drive in the cold sun, ruined only by the shock of paying £1.51 for each litre of diesel, knowing that Brian has a peculiar thirst for the stuff. We park up exactly at the spot designated by the address I entered into Homer's files and I skip across the road to the B&B opposite. The confused gentleman insists that he has no booking for me and, checking the name on my printout, I see that he is entirely correct. Cursing my befuddled brain I make the twenty-metre journey to the correct establishment and check in to a small but comfortable attic room. Soon I'm driving Brian the few miles west toward the tiny village of Cummertrees. The sun is horribly low in the sky and I can barely see the way in the fading, yet blinding, light. With the help of some directions from a local lady I park Brian and stroll up along the little row of houses by the railway, identifying my prey by the huddle of spent plastic casks in the front garden. I'm about to ring the bell when I hear a cacophony of honking geese and look up to see the sky completely filled with hundreds of birds in a mesmerising swathe of V formations, preparing for their journey north as spring beckons.

Andrew soon appears, welcomes me and takes me to see his brew kit, occupying one of his sheds. It's a modest but neatly set-up kit from which he brews his three core ales and plenty of seasonal specials. The mash tun has a sloped floor to allow gravity to do the job of sending the wort on its merry way and indeed the whole system has been cleverly set up for purpose. Andrew has no wish for expansion and tells me he has two jobs as well as his brewing duties to keep him busy. He's got a stout nearly ready to rack and orders in the pipeline that mean he'll be brewing this weekend. His enthusiasm for his craft is quite infectious and he kindly sends me on my way with a couple of bottles, one boasting 7% ABV. When I suggest I should drink that one slowly he counters that I should "get it down" me. I'm sure I will.

On our way to Annan I reflect that this first day back on the road has been really enjoyable. Three quite different breweries, a fine set of knowledgeable and engaging brewers, a clear and sunny day and Brian is performing like his hibernation had never happened. I venture out that evening in search of some tasty, cheap scran and plump for a café at the back of a chipper where I consume a decent-sized plateful of macaroni cheese pie and chips. The pie was very tasty but I'm sure it had been some time in the microwave as it was lava-hot and the texture of rubber. I ate the lot though.

After a disturbed night's sleep, due to cold feet and sub-optimal pillows, I sit alone in the breakfast room, anticipating my full vegetarian breakfast feast. The plateful doesn't in any way disappoint and I mentally chastise myself for having had the audacity to also pork my way through a plateful of Alpen and three pieces of toast and marmalade. All of the above, a nice room and free Wi-Fi mean that this has been pretty good value for a mere £30. We drive past Dumfries on our way to Castle Douglas and I spot a sign for the Sulwath Brewery, just off the main street. Allen greets me inside and I am immediately transported back to Bridge of Allan (no pun intended), such are the similarities in look and feel. Allen and I chat away about all things beer at great length while he surreptitiously draws me a tasting glass for each of the five beers on tap. It's only 10:30am but I feel it would be rude to refuse, so I slowly sip my through them all. My favourite is called Grace after the Selkirk Grace, written by Rabbie Burns and recited before the traditional haggis feast by thousands of Burns' Night hosts on each 25th January.

Our chat turns to the old chestnut of keg v cask and Allen has several anecdotes involving that theme and numerous CAMRA foot soldiers that have passed this way. Some of these troops are just a little too enthusiastic and abhor anything that comes from a keg. One chap wanted to try a beer but it was only available in keg not cask, so he opted instead for the same beer, but in a bottle. Allen laughs as he tells me that both are produced in exactly the same way. Another guy was horrified to see what he thought was a real ale being delivered from a font, not a pump. Afraid that some unsuspecting real ale buff may inadvertently order this in error, he insisted that Allen clearly mark the tap with 'KEG'. Of course, CAMRA have no authority over these things but Allen plastered the word 'keg' all over the tap and label in sarcastic obeisance.

One of the many choices facing brewers is whether to use metal or plastic casks and indeed we've touched on this already. I've heard both sides of the argument with perhaps the smaller players preferring plastic but most opting for metal. Allen reckons the extra cost (metal ones can be up to £100 each all in, plastic about a third of that) is worth it for their resilience and longevity, even at the risk of loss. To illustrate this, he has a graveyard of plastic casks out back that he is turning into occasional stools. I receive a tour of the shop, brewery and garden, from where I can see the optimistic rows of solar panels on the roof, before being taken back inside to see a pictorial history of how a once derelict building was transformed into the bar/brewery/visitor centre that we see before us today.

Slightly later than planned, we're on our way to Ayr and the brewery of the same name, squeezed into a former garage at the back of the Wellpark hotel. The hotel car park is full so I take an unscheduled tour of downtown Ayr before finding a suitable spot and strolling up to reception. I'm directed round to the tradesman's entrance but Anthony is busy finishing off a bout of cask filling so I retreat to the bar for a cheese and pineapple baguette. Andrew soon joins me and explains that he moved away from the family restaurant business a few years ago to realise his ambition of running his own brewery. A three-week course at Brewlab and some assistance from a consultant were sufficient to prime him for duty and already some expansion is being planned.

The current brewery is cramped to say the least but it clearly does the job. Adjacent to the kit is a small space acting as a cellar, without actually being a cellar as such. I realise that for all the 41 breweries that I've seen I have yet to see the multiplicity of pipes, kegs and casks that make up a cellar kit. Attached to each keg pipeline, I notice that there is a fascinating short glass tube, like something from a large chemistry set, which controls the flow in an ingenious way. When the keg contains beer the wee plug inside allows the nectar to flow through when the tap is opened in the bar. When the keg empties, the plug falls down so that the font can suck out the remains from the pipes, without creating pockets of air that would lead to a bout of coughing and spluttering at the customer delivery end. Genius.

We're pretty much done with the beer chat but not before both Anthony and hotelier Paul confess their wishes to run off with a campervan one day (not necessarily together), and on that note I run off with Brian, bound for Glasgow. Kelburn will have to wait until tomorrow as I'm late and their brewer's off early; it's all good though as they're brewing tomorrow. I'm tired and I'm facing a long evening in the Glasgow Airport Travelodge, in desolate surroundings. To cheer myself after I check in, I request a mint Magnum from the tempting vending machine, being my personal favourite ice cream on a stick. To my absolute horror, the machine instead vends a Solero Berry Explosion and doesn't even give me the extra 20p change. I feel like I'm suffering for my art tonight so once my writing chores are done I reward myself with a decent four cheese pizza and neck the 500 beer from Strathaven, while watching the new Pope emerge onto the balcony in St. Peter's Square on telly.

The next morning I spend a moment inspecting Brian and feel a touch concerned at the progress being made by the rust on his bodywork. Some major cosmetic surgery will be needed very soon if we are to have him with us long into the future. I'm also a tad crestfallen when I inspect the grey onesie bundled up within his interior as it is clearly much wetter than I had first thought and is weeping a significant puddle onto the floor. There's nothing I can do right now so I head off to my last brewery of the week, Kelburn. The short drive to Barrhead is not a pretty one and the brewery itself is located in a practical but grim location on a small industrial estate next to a bus terminus.

I park up and saunter round to unit 10 where I let myself in and find the office where Ross is working. I explain my previous chats with sister Karen who's having a day off today and, introductions made, we take a short tour of the brewery. It's a fairly standard ten-barrel set-up, recently expanded to house several fermentation vats and twelve conditioning tanks. The conditioning tank room is rather chilly so we return to the warm office for a chat about their business, the industry and all things beer. I learn that their bottling needs are met by the Isle of Skye Brewery, which seems a long way to go with, say, Sulwath just down the road. The brewery's been here for 11 years now but they first started at nearby Houston where I shall visit in due course. Ross tells me that growth has been good but has steadied a bit recently, perhaps necessitating a sales push in the near future.

It's a busy brew day for Kelburn so I bid farewell and guide Brian carefully down the narrow, busy road where I spot a sign for 'Central Laundry', housed in a fairly large building. I park Brian and pop in to see if they have a dryer big enough to take the onesie. They think they might so I drag in the wet, grey mass and deposit it in front of them. After much deliberation, unfolding, tutting and head shaking, they decide that not only is it probably too large but the material would almost certainly melt in the largest dryer. I can actually hear my bubble of optimism pop as I drag the offending item back out and drop it back inside Brian where it shall have to fester for some time longer. Soon we're at the offsite airport parking where I safely leave Brian and board the transfer bus to the airport where I have a long wait for my delayed flight. It's been a very good week though and I'm already looking forward to returning next week with a couple of mates for our weekend adventure on the isle of Arran. I wonder if they'll have any industrial-sized campervan onesie dryers there? Or maybe we can all hold it up like a sail at the back of the ferry and let the wind blow away the moisture? Yep, probably about as likely as Brian's rust magically disappearing with help from the campervan elves.

21 Arran (not)

It's early one Friday morning and my taxi driver is exclaiming his disgust with the weather, as the cold air outside becomes filled with snow, drifting gently down from an invisible source high above. We're on our way to Stansted airport but taking a slight detour that will allow us to pick up Steve and Soapy who will be joining Brian and I on our jaunt to the Isle of Arran. This island is known as 'Scotland in miniature' due to its hilly north and low-lying south and sits off the Ayrshire coast, between the mainland and the peninsula of Kintyre.

We're just slightly behind schedule as we arrive in Glasgow and transfer to the off-site parking where Brian has been awaiting my return. After brief introductions we're all loaded up with Soapy in front and Steve appearing to be miles away on the back seat, partly hidden by Brian's huge onesie, which sits in a crumpled heap on what passes as his living room floor. The first couple of attempts to spark him into life (Brian, not Steve) yield a horrible grinding whine from his rear end where his cold engine slumbers. A couple more goes with generous choke brings the splurt and vroom that herald a successful ignition mission and soon we're off, with Homer guiding us toward Ardrossan where we shall hopefully catch the lunchtime ferry so that we arrive in time for the 2pm tour at the brewery.

The weather has been a major topic of conversation among Brits since time began but these last couple of weeks it has achieved headline status due to the extreme winter conditions that are being un-seasonally visited upon us despite the calendar having reached the right side of the spring equinox. While the presence of snow last week, at the end of Brian's hibernation, caused my heart to sink, the continuation of such inclement weather puts it at risk of being scuttled. I decide to lift our spirits by introducing Brian's many features to the guys and they are clearly impressed with his phenomenal functionality. Nothing pleases them more however than the news that he is generously stocked with beers and before long they are each savouring a bottle from the Borders Brewery range. We reach the ferry terminal and I delegate checking in duties to Soapy who is handily placed where the driver would normally be positioned adjacent to the booth, which resembles an oasis of warmth in our icy desert. We're told that the ferry will have a half hour delay, which means we have an hour to hunt down some coffee and calories as well as attending to pressing bladder management issues. It does also mean however that we will be lucky to get to the Arran Brewery in time for the tour unless the captain can make up some time. Looking at the waves thrashing about on the sea and the thickening layer of snow, we adjust to the probability of deferring our brewery visit until tomorrow.

The ferry has by now arrived from Arran and is disgorging its cargo onto terra firma. A few moments later a Calmac chap taps on Brian's window and clearly has some news to share. Soapy wrestles with Brian's broken window winding handle and a cold blast fills the cockpit; but we are chilled more by the news than the air – the ferry has been cancelled due to 50mph winds out at sea. We are given the choice to wait for the next one in a couple of hours or receive a refund. Initially we plump for the former but an hour later, with conditions worsening, we conclude that it would be folly to suffer a wretch-inducing crossing only to be confined to quarters on an island that has little to offer on days when venturing outside risks hypothermia. There's also the risk of being stranded and these guys have families and jobs to think about back in London.

I pop across to the Calmac kiosk to deliver our decision and process our refund and, in our ensuing small talk, the chap glibly advises me that there is currently no power on Arran and it may be some time before this can be restored. This news rather trumps the ferry cancellation announcement made earlier and soundly dispatches any remaining second thoughts about waiting for the later crossing. I return to Brian cursing the weather and the crushing loss of the non-refundable £70 each on the hotel we had booked but at least we've saved the ferry fare, we're on dry land and we're not very far from Glasgow, where Soapy has already secured a triple room at the Airport Travelodge for a mere £38.

We head toward Glasgow, keeping an eye out on the way for a decent pub where we can grab some lunch. Actually, I'm the one with the eye looking out as the guys are employing all four of theirs scanning for our prey on their smartphones. A likely target hoves into view so I pull Brian into the car park only to discover that it's closed for refurbishment. We're pretty hungry now as the café at the ferry terminal was closed for staff lunch, at lunchtime. We're barely three hours into our weekend and we've had a ferry, a café and a pub let us down. Not to mention the weather. However, we can't really complain; Steve has been checking the news and apparently there's now no water as well as no power on Arran. We carry on with our search for food and are rewarded with a very decent lunch by the side of a roaring fire in a completely empty pub, before continuing on to our cheap digs at the Travelodge.

Our room has a settee that ingeniously converts to two single beds, complementing the standard double that Soapy has speedily claimed. Once these have been laid out, the entire floor is covered with bedding and the room resembles a posh refugee camp. Our Plan B is well developed by this stage and basically involves a cab into the West End for beer, food and a big screen on which we can watch the Scotland v Wales game that will later take place at Hampden Park on the south side of the city. We subsequently enjoy a long and boozy evening in Glasgow, featuring a miserable couple of hours watching Scotland snatch defeat from the jaws of victory on the telly, bookended by happier times in the Ubiquitous Chip and Oran Mor. During the evening we enjoy beers from Alechemy, Inveralmond and WEST, all of which receive positive feedback from the lads.

The next day we decide to head up towards Loch Lomond but not before scoffing an excellent breakfast at the St. Louis café on

Dumbarton Road. It's absolutely freezing outside and snow is falling intermittently but we are congratulating ourselves on our decision to duck out of Arran as we hear that on top of massive snow drifts, no water and total loss of power, soup kitchens are now being set up to feed the unfortunate souls trapped out there. The only silver lining would have been missing the torture of watching the game last night. We've identified a walk along a piece of the West Highland Way, near the Loch's east shore, which offers a pub lunch opportunity at its end. Despite being on a national, signposted trail we miss a turning and have to double back after hacking our way through some dense bush. We are treated to some fine views over the Loch and ahead we can see Ben Lomond, magnificent in its white, shining armour of snow, with its highest peak fading into the clouds above. The elongated walk sharpens our hunger and after a tumultuous lunch we are ready to make the return journey. Just before we leave the pub we all head to the loos. Only Soapy and I emerge and we can't find Steve until he strides out of the ladies' past a bemused young woman. Turns out he'd seen the sign for 'Laddies', misread it and assumed the other one must be the gents' but, offering a forfeit of urinals, it was of course for 'Lassies'. It's an easy mistake for any foreigner to make.

It's time to find a place to stay so we drive back to Balmaha and pop in to the Oak Tree Inn. I wanted to come here anyway, as it has recently opened a microbrewery, thus maybe saving me a trip later in the week. Thanks to an off-season half-price offer we secure three beds in the bunkroom, with en-suite and breakfast, for a mere £45. This helps put us in even better spirits, especially when we think of the cold and hungry group of three lads suffering on Arran in the parallel universe where we did take the later ferry. Even better, our hotel has a small drying room into which, with Soapy's help, we stuff Brian's onesie. It virtually consumes the entire space within, leaving little room for walkers' soggy apparel, but needs must. It turns out the brewer's not around today but unperturbed we tuck into a pint of the local stuff before exploring the wine list and making regular trips to the bar to select from their fine range of whiskies. The place is packed, with the bar, restaurant and even reception, crammed to the gunnels. This makes for a convivial atmosphere, aided by the warm fire and friendly service from Kirsty and Louise. Sleep once again comes easily, interrupted only by my ungainly exit from the top bunk, drunkenly feeling my way in the dark toward our facilities.

The next day we head across the Trossachs to Callander and manage to turn a 7k walk into an 11k outing by again missing a fairly obvious turnoff. Despite being well wrapped up our faces are freezing as the wind chill steals a few more degrees from the plummeting temperature. Safely back inside Brian, we punctuate our journey back to Glasgow with one more well-earned pub meal before I drop the guys off at Glasgow airport for their plane home. I'm staying, yet again, at the local Travelodge where I doubt they ever get such a regular visitor. It's been a great boys' weekend without resembling in the slightest the intended Arran and brewery itinerary. Indeed, of the five breweries I had targeted for this trip, I find myself with nil down and five to go. I use the evening to make plans to visit all of these in the next two days including Arran, if they're open and the ferry is running and the weather doesn't get even worse…

The next morning I've regained a strong sense of purpose and have arranged visits to Houston, Loch Lomond and Balmaha, where Brian's onesie has remained in an effort to finally get it dry. Talking of Brian, I had noticed on the drive down that he was slightly overheating and his engine was sounding a bit rough. I realised with horror and shame that I hadn't checked any of his vital fluids since picking him back up after his hibernation. I pass on breakfast to make time to attend to his needs and find that his oil's so low, it's not even registering on his dipstick. Likewise his antifreeze has almost dipped out of sight. I do my best to rejuvenate him before making the short journey west to Houston Brewery, housed within the Fox and Hounds pub. Carl is the brewer here and tells me that the brewery was created in '97 and now makes up to 70 barrels of beer each week. Such output means brewing almost every day to meet external demand, with just a fraction being sold in the attaching pub. The cellar set-up, where we're standing, is a mass of connecting pipes attached to valves on the wall, giving an impression of a giant, old-fashioned telephone exchange.

The pub has just been purchased by new owners but has been around since '79. 1779 that is. It was originally a coaching inn, offering a staging post for coaches making their way between Lanarkshire and Renfrewshire. Indeed, one of the bars is built within what clearly used to be the space used to stable the horses while the travellers refreshed themselves. Visitors these days are more likely to come from the surrounding areas and include Rangers manager Ally McCoist, who is apparently a regular and no doubt needs the odd drink given Rangers' current predicament. Having seen round the brewery Carl shows me around the pub and I spot that one hand-pull is sporting a clip featuring the 'Buddies' otherwise known as St Mirren, the local football team. This precipitates an extensive football discussion led by Dave the new owner, who has now joined us. Carl is still basking in the glory of St. Mirren's recent cup win while Dave laments the present state of Scottish football and reminisces over happier times. These are dark days for Scottish football but our beer industry seems to be booming!

On the way toward Loch Lomond Brewery, Brian and I refresh ourselves with twenty litres of diesel and a Double Decker respectively. The brewery is based on the Lomond Industrial Estate in Alexandria near Balloch at Loch Lomond's southern tip, and at the second attempt we find it. Duncan is manning the wee shop at the front, which I peruse while Fiona finishes some racking. One of the beers is called Lochtoberfest but sadly there isn't (yet) any such festival, just a German style beer with a cool name. Turns out that Fiona gave up her previous profession, (which I promised not to reveal), to set up the brewery with her hubby about a year and a half ago. It's a decent size with a ten-barrel capability but they're only brewing once a week for now while they expand their sales channels. Fiona is full of enthusiasm and energy, which is just as well with three kids as well as the brewery to run. They mostly do casks and love their real ales but also sell bottled, filtered beers. Fiona explains that "many people don't know how to handle real ale in a bottle" resulting in a cloudy beer and disappointed customers. We have a chat about Scottish brewing and she tells me that the Arran/Skye merger and planned expansion in Falkirk may be floundering due to funding being denied. I check this up online and find that the plans have indeed been dented by the refusal of funding, although not entirely abandoned. It's not been a good week for Arran.

Brian and I make our way up the east shore of Loch Lomond back to Balmaha where I check into the Oak Tree Inn for the second time in three days. After a delicious bowl of carrot, chilli and coconut soup I go to meet with David who's in charge of the small one-barrel brewery round the corner. The same family that owns the hotel also has the brewery and a shop and David tells me of plans to diversify the business and expand the brewery once a suitable location is secured. Right now he's just brewing enough for the hotel but, even in winter, it's hard to keep up with demand. Right now only the eighty shillings is on offer of the three ales normally brewed. I had tried this at the weekend and was sure that something like treacle must have been added to achieve the flavour of molasses but David assures me that it all comes from the chocolate malts in the mix. He's about to finalise the branding and soon the blandly named 'eighty shillings' will be resplendent with a new moniker, no doubt evocative of the loch-side location. There is indeed an oak tree by the entrance to the hotel and it has a large blue ribbon wrapped around it, which has firmly and annoyingly planted the 'Tie a Yellow Ribbon' song deep into my brain. Turns out though that this is to celebrate the recent birth of a baby boy in the family; different coloured ribbons have featured in the past to celebrate other big events. Perhaps they'll tie a sludge brown one there next, in honour of Brian's visit.

That evening I dine in the Oak Tree restaurant but I'm denied the chance to indulge in the fruits of the brewery next door as all three beers have now run out. I console myself with a bottle of red from Puglia, which nicely complements my goat's cheese and spinach lasagne. One bloke comes over for a chat and effervesces about his attempt to climb Ben Lomond today before having to abandon his quest due to poor visibility. I'm wondering how mad you have to be to subject yourself to such harsh conditions when he shows me a video of him jumping in the loch, protected only by his underwear, before getting dressed and going for a drive, still dripping wet. I conclude that the only thing weirder than jumping in the loch in your boxers is showing a stranger a video of that insane act.

The next morning I manage to get confirmation that the Arran Brewery is presently closed so, although the ferries are operating, I decide to postpone that trip in the hope of returning another day. This then just leaves me with the Clockwork Brewery and pub on Glasgow's south side, close to Hampden Park, scene of Friday night's miserable result. Parking spaces are in short supply so it's a long walk back to the bar, unmistakable by its iconic sign outside. The long, curving bar is festooned with a dazzling variety and number of taps and pulls, requiring a short stroll and long memory to take in the full range before making a choice. I meet with Declan, the sole brewer here, who takes me on a tour of the brewery that is hiding backstage. We have a grand old chat about all things beer and brewing in Scotland while standing in the small space that houses the mash tun and kettle. Declan tells me that he has been indulging in a bit of foraging to seek inspirational ingredients for herbal additions to a beer. He was taken by the smell and flavour of the sorrel he found and hopes to add that to a future recipe. I haven't heard yet of anyone else using sorrel and it's encouraging to still come across something new in my 46th brewery.

When we then enter the much larger space next door that houses the conditioning tanks, I'm treated to something else that I have never seen before. There are maybe a dozen of these contraptions, resembling small metal diving bells and together presenting a scene that could have graced an episode from an early Doctor Who series. Normally one would extract the matured beer from these vessels into casks or bottles before sending them off to be drained into customers' glasses. Here though, they have streamlined the process by pumping the beer directly from the tanks to the taps and pulls in the bar. The ones holding keg style beer are already under pressure as they would be in a keg, but the real ales are still fermenting so we have a CO_2 challenge to deal with. This is managed by a Heath Robinson contraption made up of long tubes, a plastic beaker with carbon in the bottom and a massive bag hanging from the ceiling. This bag is inflated and deflated to manage the optimum carbon dioxide levels in the tanks, a bit like a gas terminal moves up and down as our gas supply is pumped in and out to maintain our supplies. Just when you think you've seen it all...

Declan takes me back to the bar where he kindly pours me tasting glasses of five beers from his range. These are all pretty good and include a lager, an amber ale and my favourite of the five that has been dry hopped to produce lots of hoppy favours and aromas without too much bitterness. These retail from as little as £2.25 a pint, once again illustrating the advantage to brewer, publican and punter alike of having the end-to-end process under one roof. I thank Declan and have a quick bite to eat before returning to Brian to plan my next move. It's only 3pm, there are no more breweries to visit and I don't fancy spending the next seven or eight hours stuck in the Travelodge so I decide to take a chance that my son, Nick, will be around and could supply a free bed.

I make the 50-mile journey to Auld Reekie (aka Edinburgh) only to find he's on night shift and his girlfriend is ill so, after a pleasant catch up, I'm back in Brian and heading for that Travelodge again! My sleeping arrangements have been rather strange this week: Travelodge, Balmaha, Travelodge, Balmaha, Travelodge! It's dark as I prepare to head back west and when I switch on Brian's headlights it appears that only one of the circular displays in front of me is being illuminated. This means that I can't read the speedometer and Brian looks like he's wearing an eye patch. I mentally add this fault to our growing repair list before pressing on to my familiar resting place in time to see Scotland lose (again) to Serbia and make some plans for the weeks ahead before retiring. While carrying out my research I find news of more new breweries opening up across the land, threatening to create a never-ending journey for Brian and I on our perpetual quest.

After a decent sleep and leftover pizza for breakfast I check his oil again and glug in another pint or so to keep him topped up. I make a mental note to find a large, dry space on which I can fold up and put away his onesie but it does seem to at least be a little dryer now. I leave Brian in the desolate, remote parking lot and make my way back home, already anticipating an exciting trip to Colonsay next week.

Steve and Soapy wondering

how far it is to the next pub

22 Scotland Sale

You're probably thinking that that should have read 'Scotland's Ale' and I would have to agree entirely. It's just a slight sleight of punctuation but of course it changes the meaning entirely. We shall however explore both versions of the punctuation in this chapter. One of the questions I wanted to answer on my journey was how ales in Scotland differ from those south of the border. Was there anything special that one could associate with Scottish beers that would set them aside from beers brewed anywhere else in the world? As you will know, only whisky distilled in Scotland can be deemed as Scotch; everywhere else it's just plain old whisky or whiskey.

Beer, however, is much too ubiquitous for any particular country, never mind Scotland, to claim dibs on it and give it a unique marque. That said, if any country resonates with the word 'ale' it would be England (at least in my mind). So, is there anything that sets English ale apart from its international cousins? Is it the only place where the customer asks for a pint of mild, bitter or best? Do these terms even mean anything in any other country? Certainly in Scotland I have never ordered a beer using any of the above. A pint of heavy, special or anything from 60 to 90 shillings are the orders that are typically belched out at a traditional Scottish pub. So, is 'bitter' best or is 'heavy' really special? How did brewing evolve and how did we get to where we are today? How would you recognise a Scottish beer in a blind tasting like a wine expert would tell apart a Rioja from a Bordeaux? Before we get too deeply into Scotland's ales, let's spend some time on the Scotland sale.

It's not possible to research a book about Scottish beers at this point in history without making some mention of 'CAMSI', or the CAMpaign for Scottish Independence. I don't think CAMSI actually exists but it will do as a virtual body to encapsulate all those factions in favour of separation. This is a topic that has been around throughout my life but gained momentum when the Scottish Parliament was created in 1999 and again when the SNP (Scottish National Party) took control of that vehicle in 2007. That year had great meaning in itself, being exactly 300 years since the Act of Union brought Scotland together with England and Wales to form Great Britain, which later evolved into the United Kingdom when Northern Ireland was annexed in 1922. On October 15 2012, while merrily scooting around Scotland in Brian, agreement was reached (between Prime Minister Cameron and First Minister Salmond, not me and Brian) that there would be a vote for Scottish Independence in autumn 2014. The timing was again auspicious because that year will celebrate the 700th anniversary of the battle of Bannockburn, where the Scots' armies were victorious over King Edward's army ("and sent him homeward to think again", as the lyrics of Flower of Scotland tell us).

This time around though, voters not soldiers will decide the outcome but, as I write, a victory for the nationalists is not expected.

Interestingly, the vote is being given to all those aged 16 and over in Scotland at the date of the referendum. Extending the voting age to 16 from 18 was a departure for UK elections but of more interest was the fact that non-Scots living in Scotland (however briefly) would be allowed to participate in determining our future, while Scots living outside Scotland (however briefly) would not. This is definitely significant as I suspect that one grows more romantically connected to one's country of birth the more one lives away from it. If we consider also that ex-pats wouldn't have to live with the practical impact of separation, and temporary residents may not greatly care to make it happen, then this eligibility delineation probably isn't helping the cause. But these are the buyers who must decide whether we make the purchase now that the UK Government has put Scotland 'up for sale'.

The UK is a strange creation indeed. Our passports tell us that we are from the United Kingdom of Great Britain and Northern Ireland. When someone asks you which country you're from, what do you say? UK? Britain? *Great* Britain? Or do you immediately associate yourself with England, Scotland, Wales or Northern Ireland? I often find that even British people don't exactly know the difference between GB and UK. And don't even get me started on the American habit of referring to Britain as England. Great Britain is simply the biggest island of the British Isles, which include Ireland. I'm not sure how to define Britain (as opposed to Great Britain) or how exactly to explain British, other than in our stereotypical characteristics and behaviours. When did Wales stop being a principality and start being a country? Is Northern Ireland a province, region or country? Is Scotland a country? The definition of 'country' says "A nation with its own government, occupying a particular territory." A 'nation' is defined as "A large aggregate of people united by common descent, history, culture, or language, inhabiting a particular country or territory." This would lead me to a statement that may shock: 'England is not a country!' Indeed, Liechtenstein is more of a country than England. So, where are the calls for English independence? If we are to break up the union that has had an incredibly successful 300 years shouldn't we all have a say in that? Taking Scotland out of the UK leaves a very odd looking map and doesn't leave a great deal of land outside of England (with due respect to our fellow Celts). Can you still call a Kingdom 'united' that has just lost a fairly sizeable chunk? You certainly couldn't describe what would remain as including 'Great Britain' as a chunk of that island has just declared UDI! Would Scotland's departure precipitate the breaking up of the remainder? Has anyone thought about the consequences beyond Scotland of Scotland's independence, should that actually happen?

I've spoken to very many people from various walks of life about Scottish independence and most of them feel it's a waste of time, will cause bad feeling between us and England, leave us all worse off and take ages to implement. The same people mostly agree that there's little chance of it actually happening. I've yet to meet anyone in favour who has compelling arguments to show that this will be better for Scotland, but some have argued convincingly that we probably won't be any worse off. I can't imagine that William Wallace would have got very far if instead of saying "they will never take our freedom", he'd said "they will never make us no worse off"! In truth, the most passionate arguments in favour tend to follow from history and to almost the same degree, football. The history part is quite understandable given that we used to be an independent nation and had many battles with the English over several centuries. These battles were however as much to do with money, land and power as national identity. Sport offers some fine examples of our strange make-up. In the Olympics we compete as Great Britain but, contrary to my descriptions above, our team includes athletes from Northern Ireland so shouldn't we be calling ourselves the UK team? When we compete in the Commonwealth Games however, we send along teams from each of the four home nations. In rugby, the Ireland team represents the whole island, combining the independent Republic as well as the wee British piece at the top. As for football, there were great howls of derision from all home nations bar England when it was announced that there would be a GB football team taking part. This worked fine for the women's game but was considered an outrage for the men's game, by the Scots in particular. Nationalism is never felt as keenly on any front as it is on the football park. That hasn't stopped us in the past, however, scouring the globe for quality players whom, by some quirk of fate, may have had a Scottish granny and would therefore qualify to play for Scotland – even if they were Englishmen!

I personally think that Scotland's status is only part of the issue and that there are some bigger questions to be answered. The vote that I would like to see offered to the people of the UK would be to decide the following question: 'Should we dissolve the Union and operate as four separate countries with our own Governments or should we forget the constituent parts and just call ourselves Britain?' I always find it a bit confusing, filling in immigration forms while flying to another country, when you have to put 'UK' for country of origin but 'British' for nationality. Right now I'm Scottish and British (and European) and come from the UK. How much easier would it be if I could say that I'm British from Britain or indeed Scottish from Scotland? It seems like we've been in a 300 year engagement but the bride doesn't want to get married and have to change her name.

So, if we're going to vote for anything then let's go the whole hog and sort this out properly, at least for the next 300 years. Better than that, let's not bother at all because why would you fix something that doesn't seem broken right now? Why even bother arguing about borders and names and history when our nation is full of people who are definitely not "united by common descent, history, culture, or language" and all the better for it. In a world where global corporations seem to hold as much or even more sway over our lives than do Governments, what importance should we be attaching to whether we're Scottish or British, Catalan or Spanish, Bavarian or German? Breaking up a successful union seems like, at best, a distraction when we're already struggling with creating a bigger, less valuable and more challenging union with our friends in Europe. Let's just get on with sorting out the really important stuff that will remain however we describe our boundaries and make time to share a few beers together without getting heavy or bitter.

So, from the Scotland sale to Scotland's ale. What, if anything, is definitively Scottish about Scottish ales and different to English ales? I asked this question of many brewers and the answers ranged from "we're using more hops than before" to "almost no difference at all these days" to "maybe we like them a bit sweeter". Sweeter would be no surprise at all as we do love our confections and no main course, however large, would ever be allowed to get in the way of dessert. I could never quite grasp the logic of being told "clear your plate or there won't be any dessert for you". This would most likely cause the child (aka me) to be too full for dessert but determined nonetheless to eat it all having earned that right. And we're definitely not talking sorbet or fresh fruit salad here, as dessert would indubitably involve some form of pastry or sponge and great dollops of custard. Perhaps in health conscious households of today the plea would be more "you'd better clear your plate if you're hungry because there certainly isn't any dessert".

The first beers I enjoyed were also sweet, specifically Sweetheart Stout, originally brewed by George Younger, but now part of Tennent's. As well as being sweet this was pretty low alcohol so perfect as an introduction to beer. I suspect if I were to try it again now, it wouldn't be to my liking at all. I recall it tasting like slightly alcoholic Soda Stream Cola, but back then it made me feel like a man. The picture of the woman on the can enhanced that feeling of becoming grown up; a quite iconic image of a lady called Venetia Stevenson. The same picture has been used for over 50 years, having started in 1958, and may have been the inspiration for the emergence of the Tennent's lager lovelies. Forgive me the slight digression but there's a good story here. Venetia was born in England in 1938 before moving to America to become a model and actress. Her second marriage was to Don Everly of the Everly Brothers and her daughter is the subject of Sweet Child o' Mine by Guns 'n' Roses, having been married to Axl Rose. So I guess she did all right after her career peaked so early when she posed for that photo, frozen in time, at twenty years of age. I'm actually surprised that this 'beer' is still for sale, being such a dated concoction, but you can still see it sometimes on supermarket shelves and I guess therefore someone out there is still buying Sweetheart Stout, whether for the picture on the can or the contents within.

In my humble experience I would say that English ales are broadly bitterer than those I tasted in Scotland but this is a huge generalization across multiple styles of beer. I do think however that a traditional pint of English bitter does taste different to its nearest equivalent in Scotland. The experience of drinking it certainly feels different when you're stood on the street, outside the pub, with the sun shining down, blocking the way of innocent passers by. English pubs do also have a particular atmosphere that you don't often find anywhere else. In recent times there has been a clear trend in Scotland to create more hoppy beers and hoppier beers, reflecting the perceived demand from the market. With so many English folk living in Scotland and vice versa, tastes are spreading and merging. Possibly of greater importance is the number of English people acting as head brewers in Scotland. Over one in three of the brewers I met were from south of the border. I'm sure this was precipitated by a lifestyle decision but when you see how geographically concentrated breweries are in England (as is the population) then you can understand why you may choose to set up in Scotland where it's still possible to be 50 miles from your nearest competitor. Maybe the relative isolation of

breweries in Scotland affects the nature of the product and its
individuality more than them being Scottish per se. Take the Valhalla
Brewery as an example, located far away up on the isle of Unst. Their
influences are probably more Norse than Scottish, illustrated by their
use of the Bere strain of barley in making one of their range of beers.
Incidentally, I've just read that Bere is pronounced 'bear' whereas I
heard the Shetlanders called it 'berr' - another fine example of their
weird but wonderful accent.

So, what else might affect the nature of Scottish beers? Water
would be one example and we covered that in an earlier chapter. What
about the climate – does that make a difference? Well, it certainly did
historically as, since hops couldn't be grown in Scotland, they tended
not to be used in our beers until sometime around the Act of Union in
1707. It's not that the weather suddenly improved at that point but I
imagine signing up as mates would have made importing English hops
a lot easier. Other plants such as heather or bog myrtle were until then
used in place of hops in Scotland but I imagine that these probably
didn't impart quite the same level of bitterness. I've only once had a
pint of Fraoch Ale so I really can't point to any personal field research
on this matter. Yet. The weather may well also make a difference to
our tastes in beer, just as it influences our preferences for food. It's
well documented that the Scottish diet is one of the most unhealthy,
fat-fuelled examples in Europe. There may be many reasons for this
including cultural, social and financial but I'm quite certain that some
of the blame must go to the dreich weather. I'm not going to explain
what 'dreich' means to the un-initiated as it is superbly onomatopoeic.
You just don't fancy a salad in cold, windy, driving rain and, by the

same token, I would opt for a rich, dark, sweet ale over a hoppy, light beer when the rain is cascading down and the wind is howling a gale.

While our tastes may be fusing somewhat for the reasons given earlier, I do believe that some differences will remain, driven perhaps partly by the rejection of English terminology in calling ales: mild, bitter or best. You may find the odd guest English ale in an Edinburgh pub that has the word 'bitter' attached to it but it's a rare sight. Contrast and compare with English pubs where you're unlikely to ever find a bar that doesn't offer at least one beer with that moniker on display. It's almost synonymous with ale or beer in some quarters. These arguments are perhaps all rather academic in any case as the big brands that dominate the market are consumed in most parts of the world, never mind across our wee island. So I would have to conclude that the main thing that makes Scottish ales Scottish is that they're brewed in Scotland. (That was worth waiting for wasn't it?) An Englishman may have brewed them, they may have English hops in the recipe and they may very well be sold and drunk extensively in England, but if they're created in Scotland then Scottish ales they most certainly are!

23 Colonsay

Preparing for this particular journey was a lot of fun. My first decision, once initial contact had been made with the brewery, was whether to take the ferry or fly. I've been on quite a few ferry trips during this tour and given that the island is rather small (about eight miles by two), there wasn't going to be a great demand for Brian's services. In fact, taking Brian at all would have proved a bit of a mission as you can't take a campervan on the ferry without permission from the Colonsay Community Council – so I would have needed mission permission. This is to prevent anyone from free camping on the island and therefore, to get clearance to ship a Brian, one has to be able to prove that accommodation has been booked. Well, if I have to book accommodation anyway then Brian definitely gets a couple of days off. So the ferry wasn't going to be necessary but it still offered a very pleasant and cheap way to get me to Colonsay. The flying option was much more attractive though and at £65 return it was impossible to resist. Even better, the flights I chose had to go via Islay, both there and back, so it was like getting two for the price of one. Yes, I am a bit of an aeroplane anorak and was pretty excited about getting on the wee twin propeller 8-seater at Oban airport.

The planning had only just begun. There's only one hotel on the island and although it's very handily placed close to the brewery (and the ferry terminal) it was a bit expensive for my tastes. There were a few B&Bs but I was surprised and delighted to find that Colonsay has a backpacker lodge. I called up the Estate to ask about availability and the helpful Irina confirmed that I could have a twin room for £22 a night and if I were lucky, no one else would be sharing it. I could have gone for the bothy or the dorm but the few pounds difference in price seemed like a good deal for the significant increase in comfort. I needed transport to get me the 4 miles from the airport (aka landing strip) to the lodge and Irina helpfully suggested that I call Kevin who was apparently on taxi duty these days, there being no public transport. I then asked about bikes and was told that Archie could sort me out as he kept bikes all over the island but needed a bit of notice. The lodge is in the middle of nowhere (actually the whole island is in the middle of nowhere) and has no food or drink but does offer facilities for cooking if you bring your own food. The nearest (only) place to get a bite of dinner most evenings is the aforementioned hotel, imaginatively called the Colonsay Hotel, about two miles away, so the bike would definitely come in handy for that too. The only shop on the island looked like it would be closed before I would arrive so I'd have to plan in advance to take some supplies with me just in case the weather should make cycling in the dark to the hotel along unlit roads, inadvisable. I'd almost forgotten that I was going over there to visit the brewery!

I always get a buzz from visiting any new island but Colonsay gets extra points for being home to the brewery whose website provided a catalytic moment in my deciding to write this book. I've also managed to get an appointment with Glenfinnan after several failed attempts last autumn, so I'm pretty excited about the week ahead. Even this latest effort seemed to be doomed however, as the only day they're around is Wednesday, which I'm already committed to spend on Colonsay. In a final throw of the dice I arranged for Joan, who lives by the brewery, to receive me and show me around. Having both of these elusive targets on my itinerary for this week already feels like an achievement as I arrive in Glasgow and make my way to pick Brian up. As I stroll across the car park I feel a strange warmth on my face and there's an unfamiliar light in my eyes. After months of freezing weather and the coldest Easter ever, it's taking a few moments for me to adjust to this sudden climatic change. Could this really be a first taste of spring sunshine – in Glasgow? As if to echo the coming of spring a rejuvenated Brian starts first time but, in his excitement, simultaneously pollutes half the car park with an impressive burst of bluish-white smoke. Homer guides us out of Glasgow, across the Erskine Bridge and up through Argyll to our first destination of the week, Oban.

To keep me amused on the journey I am treating my ears to the latest musical cornucopia offered by my friend Scott's 'top tens of the year' series. He's been doing this pretty much since we met back in the 90s and while I try to reciprocate, he is the master. I presently have his 'top ten albums' CD bounding merrily from Brian's speaker system and we're counting down to the number one album, which this year is by Alt-J. While they were overjoyed with their Mercury Music award, I hear that they are also deeply touched by this accolade. I shall later explore the top ten singles before indulging in Scott's top ten covers of the year. Before long we've escaped the confines of

Glasgow's conurbation and are making our way up the west side of Loch Lomond. This affords me incredible views of the mountains that are wrapped around the far side of the loch, each still displaying evidence of previous heavy snowfalls. Some are completely hidden beneath their white sheath, some retain only a cropped topping while others must have natural under-soil heating as only a scattering of dots and patches of snow remain. Today is the last day of the Easter weekend so there is a procession of motorhomes and caravans making their way back to civilisation from whichever highland retreat they had chosen to spend their weekend at, no doubt gnawing hungrily through the cold, hard chocolate of their Easter eggs. I can almost see the disappointment on their faces as they curse the sun for it's cruel timing, shining warmly through their windscreens as they contemplate the return to work tomorrow. I am also disappointed that, despite having my eyes peeled and right arm at the ready, there are no Brians retreating south to whom I can send a friendly wave.

Homer is still resolutely on GMT despite the clocks having moved forward last weekend. I can sympathise with him somewhat as the whole daylight saving thing seems tiresome and unnecessary. Before I realise his mistake though, I am surprised to feel such hunger pangs at this apparently early hour but, reassured that lunchtime is indeed upon us, I decide on a stop at Tyndrum, gateway to the western highlands. After my welcome pause for refreshment we head for Oban and are finally rewarded with another Brian passing us by and his human keepers all wave merrily back at me in time honoured fashion. Our route essentially follows the railway line that takes passengers from Glasgow to Oban through Glen Lochy. This is one of my most favourite train journeys ever but the other branch of the West Highland line that goes up to Fort William and Mallaig, once voted the best train journey in the world, possibly eclipses it. If you've never done this before, choose a clear, sunny day, take a picnic, book window seats and pop open the wine. Once you get past the neds drinking Buckfast on the outskirts of Glasgow, the scenery is breath taking. I recommend that lovers of rail travel check out the excellent 'Man in Seat 61' website for more tantalising information.

By now the weather had further improved and the sky was almost entirely blue, with the sunlight twinkling and glistening on the snow. We soon arrive in Oban and I park Brian up overlooking Oban Bay from where we can hear the safety announcements being made on the Mull ferry docked half a mile around the shorefront. The Cuan Mor pub and restaurant sits on the main road looking out across the harbour toward the tiny island of Kerrera, with Mull offering a stunning backdrop. I step inside and enquire after my host, Findlay, and I am taken through to the hidden world behind the bar that once housed a nightclub but now contains an eerily empty and silent function suite behind which is the brewery, nestled in its self-contained space. Findlay, it transpires, was an engineering graduate who went to work at Heinz but as he liked beer more than tomato sauce he did a post-grad year at Heriot-Watt and landed the job here at Oban Bay Brewery. In addition to their own beers, they also brew the range that was formerly created on the Isle of Mull before both businesses were combined under one roof. The beers sell out front but also find their way to several other outlets around Argyll and Lochaber. The winters bring both a huge fall in demand for beer and bitterly cold temperatures in the brewery. More challenging though is the opposite summer combination of high demand and high temperatures, necessitating the creation of a cooling cupboard built to ensure the beers can condition properly before being released to a thirsty public.

Findlay has a few bottles left over from a tasting so he furnishes me with three of those, two from the Mull range and one from Oban Bay called 'Skelpt Lug', (which translates as slapped ear), that I shall add to Brian's clinking, clanking collection. I venture back through the bar and outside to the small patio that today provides an excellent suntrap. Incredibly, I can even remove my jacket as I sit back, stretch out and savour the pint of Oban Bay Skinny Blonde that I have, moments earlier, procured from the bar. It's ostensibly a soaring 7° Celsius but it feels warmer as I motionlessly soak up the rays. Thirst quenched, I take a wander around town and check out the various eating opportunities but decide in the end to return to Cuan Mor, this time opting for the interior warmth as the sun is slowly disappearing behind the hills to the west as the earth continues its relentless, rotational routine. I still feel a tad guilty when I opt for fish and chips, having been so long a determined vegetarian, but I know it's going to be fresh and tasty here and I'm not disappointed. My second pint of Skinny Blonde does an excellent job of lubricating my repast but I resist the temptation of the substantial sticky toffee pudding. Instead I hike up the hill to my room from which there are stunning views of the fading sunset.

I'm up and away early the next morning, headed for Fort William where I shall be meeting John from the Glenfinnan Brewery. I want to get there early both to score some brekkie but also to try and give poor Brian a proper wash, which he is desperately in need of. Unfortunately, he's too tall for the automatic car wash and the jet wash isn't yet open so we muckily repair to the Morrison's café for some scran. The vegetarian breakfast bizarrely excludes the vegetarian sausages that are listed under 'extras' so I decide to ask for a vege sausage roll. I've already messed up the simple act of getting myself a coffee by selecting the wrong size of cup and creating a small cappuccino lake in the tray under the dispenser, so I approach the unsmiling assistant with some trepidation. "Can I have vegetarian sausages on a roll please" I enquire. A grunt of affirmation is offered in reply but I'm assuming this delicacy will be made-to-measure rather than off the peg so I ask about the size of the roll, therefore enabling me to choose the appropriate amount of sausages with which to fill it. I am informed that it is a 'normal' roll so, none the wiser, I opt for three sausages, just to make sure. "You only get two" she bawls in response, instantly closing the conversation and confirming the utter pointlessness of the previous roll-scale conversation. It was actually rather tasty though after all of that. I was however amused while eating to overhear a waitress tell a table that although they did have eggs available, they only had fried not scrambled – go figure!

So that we may recognise each other, John has informed me that he will be in a blue Berlingo. Now, I am completely out of touch with car names and designs so I had at first assumed he was describing his designer Italian overcoat rather than his Citroen van. Luckily a spot of Googling had put me right on that one. Our meeting is successfully executed as planned, next to the recycling bins in the Lidl car park and soon we're on our way. As we drive we talk about the bush fire that had broken out nearby the day before, which explains the procession of fire engines I had observed from my room. For an area normally drenched in rain year round this was somewhat ironic and made the national news. The scenery peaks as we pass the head of Loch Shiel where the Glenfinnan Monument stands in homage to the place where Bonnie Prince Charlie raised his standard at the beginning of the Jacobite rebellion in 1745. The view down the loch is never anything other than stunning, but especially so on a day like this. We're soon at the brewery where we meet with Joan who is preoccupied with grandchildren duties. John shows me around the brewery and I learn some new stuff about casks. Apparently, in Scotland, these are typically stored vertically in the cellar, whereas the English prefer theirs to be horizontal – so we stand up while they lie down. This of course means that different methods are deployed for managing and accessing the beer through the various holes. We talk about the risks of losing casks and despite Glenfinnan's being labelled, numbered and carefully tracked by John, these can still go missing. One actually turned up in Bristol, hunted down by a company called Kegwatch, and I wonder how long it will be before a trackable microchip is embedded in each cask. Like any small brewery, there are many challenges to be overcome to maintain the equipment in prime condition, using whatever materials and labour come most easily to hand. One particular challenge here however seems to be the proliferation of midges in the midsummer months, with John describing the opening to the brewery as being like magnetic north in its attractiveness to the tiny, biting pests.

Joan has kindly invited us inside for a coffee and biscuit and therein we meet with her husband Dugald. I explain my purpose and he retorts with mention of Raw Spirit. I confirm this was indeed an inspiration for my present quest and he tells me that he actually gets a mention in the book, referred to as 'DJ'. This would not be the last time that Iain Banks would feature in this week's journey.

I thank Joan for the refreshments and take John back to his Berlingo before making my way to Oban airport where my flight to Colonsay awaits. The journey takes me through Benderloch, a favourite family caravan holiday spot from my childhood. Distracted by my memories, I have to swerve and brake to avoid a suicidal sheep before turning off the road and parking Brian by the tiny terminal. I'm early, it's sunny and dry and there's plenty space in the car park so I decide to spread out his onesie, fold it up and stuff it back into its sack. My geometrical estimations and folding technique are both below par but I get an acceptable result and shove the huge package to the back of Brian's attic. The lady at check-in informs me that we have a full flight this afternoon, meaning that eight of us will be squeezing onto the plane. The fire crew keep themselves busy by loading the bags and in no time we're noisily speeding down the runway and up into the welcoming blue sky. The colours offered by the tiny islands below, the turquoise sea and the submerged rocks are already captivating me when we seem to be turning around, back toward the airport. The pilot's purpose is not however to make a forced landing but rather to circle the huge sperm whale in the sea directly below us, so that we may observe this biblical beast in all its glory. Hard to top a view like that but I'm in need of a neck massage as I twist my head in every direction to take in the stunning sights around us as we buzz along just a quarter mile high.

We make our scheduled stop on Islay then hop back to Colonsay where our approach takes us over coastline that presents sea, beach and land in concentric curves of sapphire, sand and scrub. I emerge from the plane and soon spot an older gentleman standing by a bike. "You must be Archie" I say with confidence, but he responds with a bluff "no". I turn to seek out an alternative man/bike combo but he quickly confesses his cruel joke to this gullible, mainland city boy. I set off on the bike only to find the seat is ridiculously low and it's in first gear. I must look quite hilarious but rather than stop to make adjustments in front of the locals, I bravely keep going until normality can be restored in some privacy.

I've come prepared with two instant porridge pots and enough pasta/pesto for two dinners but I check out the hotel and the Pantry café anyway before continuing my journey to the backpacker lodge at the north end of the island. Looking out toward the east I can see the magnificence of the Paps of Jura standing tall and proud. Colonsay is quite lovely, with its rugged interior, fabulous coastline and lots of open space supporting a mere 120 or so residents. The lodge is at the end of a rough track and, typical of small islands, there's not a lock or key anywhere in sight. There's not another soul around right now either so I make my way in, make my bed then cycle my way back

211

along undulating roads to the island's hub, Scalasaig, where I settle down at the Colonsay Hotel. They sell the locally brewed beer here of course but disappointingly there's none on tap so I settle for a bottle of the IPA, which sets me up nicely for a glass of Nero d'Avola and dinner. I like the hotel and the staff are friendly but the risotto is possibly the most bland thing I have eaten in years. A fellow diner concurs and the offending item is struck from my bill. It's very dark outside now and bitterly cold so I decide to don my head torch and carefully wind my way back to the lodge. The clear sky above reveals a plethora of stars and the longer I look the more that they seem to fill the blackness between them with countless celestial bodies. The heating's off in the lodge so it's icy in my room but if I hide under the blankets it's just about bearable. Before nodding off I reflect on how, months ago, I started this long journey at the autumn equinox, paused it at the winter solstice, recommenced just before the spring equinox and will complete the book sometime around the summer solstice. These astronomical thoughts still my mind long enough for the warm liquid of sleep to envelop me.

I awake to a stunning morning and can't wait to get on my bike to explore the island before meeting the folks at the brewery later this afternoon. There's basically one circular road to follow but with offshoots at the north and south ends of the island. I first venture north and soon pause to ooh and aah over the lambs playing together while the mums munch the dry grass. As I'm watching, the lambs very suddenly and almost exactly in unison make a beeline for their respective maternal, mobile feeding stations and get stuck in. It was quite as if there had been some signal, a dinner bell audible only to sheep, that triggered this Pavlovian response. I leave them to their liquid lunch and press on round a corner where I see a view so stunning I have to stop and stare. The pale sand of the wide, flat beach in front of me meets the turquoise water in an arc, beyond which one can see the distant mountains of Mull on the horizon. I explore the shoreline in the warmth of the sun as the sparkling, clear water tempts me to numb myself in its icy trap. My reverie is broken by the sounds of a family cascading down to the beach from the cottages above, so I remount my two-wheeled steed and head south.

I grab a picnic lunch from the café and cycle to the bottom of Colonsay where a causeway appears at low tide, allowing walkers to visit the neighbouring island of Oransay without dampening their feet. It's so silent here that I can hear the creak of a bird's wing high above me as I look out across the sandy spar. My thoughts are preoccupied with the news I have just picked up online that Iain Banks has terminal cancer. His book, Raw Spirit, provided the inspiration for the book you're now reading. The story behind the brewery here on Colonsay provided the catalytic moment that made me believe there was a book worth writing about Scottish beer. Therefore hearing of this sad news on this island on a day as beautiful as this one provides me with an epiphany about my life. I had been seriously considering going back to work in an office after this journey is over and just two days ago an opportunity came my way, but now I know that will never happen. I want to travel and write, learn and explore, wherever that takes me.

As much as I'm loving just being on Colonsay, I am here to see a brewery and at 4pm I meet up with Sheena who shows me around the shiny brew kit in the spotless premises. Had it not been for the abandonment of Arran, this would have been my 50th brewery, which would have seemed an appropriate way to reach my half-century. As it is though, it's great to meet Chris and Bob, the "10% of the island's population" referred to on their bottles and website. Chris offers a qualification to this statistic as, with a population of about 120, they more accurately represent perhaps 10% of the adult male working population over 40. Adding all that to the marketing material would somewhat dilute its impact though. The brewery closes in winter so it's really just getting going again ahead of the summer season. This explains the lack of beers on tap at the hotel up the road. In order to meet peaks in customer demand, Chris has previously used the Isle of Skye Brewery for extra capacity but Colonsay use dried yeast and hop pellets, neither of which is normally called upon at Skye. This meant that a method had to be invented that would filter out the spent pellets, to create a clear beer and less mess. The solution was to put them into a hessian sack that was then inserted into the kettle. Great idea but I might have favoured a hemp sack myself.

Back in the shop, I'm looking around the promotional goodies and spot a certificate on the wall, proclaiming that Colonsay is indeed the smallest island in the world with its own brewery. Sheena tells me that one day some time ago, three German chaps dropped in to present the certificate personally, having done the research into the top ten such islands. This must have been a great moment for all concerned. You may be interested to know that Rarotonga in the Cook Islands came second and Bordoy in the Faroe Islands came third. Arran, Orkney and

Islay also featured in the top ten, adding up to quite a spectacular success story for Scotland in this 'niche within a niche' competition! Sheena gives me a taste of their lager, which is low on gas and high on taste and refreshment. Apparently some time ago they got a call from an Indian restaurant in London that had somehow got a hold of some of their bottles of lager and they reckoned that this would provide an excellent accompaniment to their curries. I would completely agree but unfortunately the scale of supply they required was beyond the means of Colonsay's production so they had to sadly decline. If only Sheena could remember the name of that restaurant! While the sun remains in the sky I decide to cycle back up the hill to the hotel so that I can have a bottle each of the lager and eighty shillings before heading back to base for pasta/pesto and a drop of red wine. I have a brief chat with the two painters who are spending several weeks on the island, freshening up the holiday cottages, working long hours and suffering the cold nights in the bothy. They head off to shoot some rabbits and I head off to bed.

The next day is just as stunning as the previous two and I arrive early at the landing strip to be met by Chris the brewer who also works here at the airport. The flight back offers yet more vertiginous views of the many islands but our friend the sperm whale is nowhere to be seen. I give Brian a large glug of oil before making my way to Morrison's at Fort William for another Quorn sausage sandwich. Brian desperately needs a wash but before I spot a suitable venue for his ablutions, I catch sight of two weary looking hitchhikers, smiling hopefully as we pass by. I make a spur of the moment decision and stop to pick them up. They're a French couple heading to

Newtonmore, which is the wrong side of Loch Ness for me, but in the spirit of the Auld Alliance I take them straight to their digs, present them with a free beer and continue north to catch my plane. I find a luxury jet wash near the airport that incorporates multi-coloured foam and I can almost hear Brian sigh in relief as I wash away the grime and leave him once more sparkling clean. It's been a fabulous week and the sun is still shining as I stroll across the tarmac to board my flight home.

Ready to hop to Colonsay via Islay

24 Seven

The week ahead is potentially thick with breweries. There are two that have sprung into life since I was last in the northeast and six that, for various reasons, I was unable to visit last time around. In my preparations I have contacted six of these eight targets thus far and have received three positive responses, one refusal (BrewDog) and two have yet to reply. I guess it's a start at least. My child-filled flight has delivered me to Inverness from where it's a short drive east to Forres where one of the newest breweries in Scotland, Speyside Craft, is based within a small industrial unit on the edge of town. Having missed out on Arran last week, I can announce to the head guy, Seb, that his brewery has the honour of being the point at which I achieve my half-century landmark – perhaps I should have prepared a certificate to present him with. His strapline here is 'Against the Grain', reflecting his use of barley and other cereals for making beer in an area famous for its many distilleries, linked together by the 'Whisky Trail' so favoured by tourists in these parts. His range includes a refreshing lager, citrusy IPA and a Scottish bitter, differentiated from its English cousins by a sweeter taste enabled through less hops and therefore less bittering.

Seb spends a lot of his time on sales and indeed the brewery remains open at the weekend, selling bottles from the small shop. As a local, Seb feels that Moray (pronounced to rhyme with 'furry' not 'foray') doesn't get quite the same attention as its larger neighbours, Aberdeenshire and Inverness-shire, but resisted naming his brewery after the region, preferring to save that honour for one of his beers. I try all three of his products and they do go down rather nicely. Seb's description of craft beers is that they must be created for flavour ahead of profit and we debate whether the mega-brewers could ever make that leap. We continue our bout of beer chat and I learn that the thicker head on his beers comes from the addition of 'torrified' wheat – essentially wheat that has been 'popped' rather than malted. Next time you go to the cinema, try asking for some torrified corn and see what reaction you get.

It's time to head off toward Lossiemouth where I shall kip for the night. On the way out of town I pass the football ground of the local Highland League team, Forres Mechanics; perhaps the only team that has a name with that particular suffix. I stop for a coffee en-route and call a garage in Dundee that I am hoping will be able to fix Brian's growing rust problem and give him a fresh coat of paint. The chap I speak to says rather unhelpfully that "rust is a problem" but agrees to take a look later this week. This is not good news as Brian isn't getting any younger and some reconstructive surgery is definitely needed. I continue on to Lossiemouth, settle into my B&B, take a walk around the windy shore and grab a bite to eat in the Skerry Brae, where I shall be meeting Al, co-owner of the Windswept Brewery that I shall be visiting the next morning. I know from my research that this is a brewery that eschews the use of isinglass, believing that cloudy beers are much more natural than fishy beers. I have to express my empathy with this view as watching the milky substance being poured into a cask of fine ale one time, did make me wince a bit. The more breweries I see the more I am of the opinion that quality, natural ingredients combined with excellent brewmanship are what really count. Whether real or not, howsoever carbonated and independent of the vessel from which it is served. I would unashamedly declare myself a supporter of hop flowers not pellets, live yeast and as few other ingredients, additives and fining agents as possible. I guess I would add that the less filtering and pasteurising that goes on, the better. There now, my colours are well and truly nailed to the mast.

The Skerry Brae has run out of both its Windswept beers so I am reduced to a half pint of Guinness to keep me company before Al arrives. Continuing my homework, I see that they have installed a ten-barrel brewery on the edge of town but also have a 'pilot' brewery. Given that Al and partner Nige are both ex RAF pilots I find this unintentional pun deeply amusing. Al arrives to rouse me from my private mirth and suggest that we repair to the Golf Club where it is likely that their Blonde will be on tap. Our beer talk sustains us through our first pint of Blonde but it's been inexpertly poured and is nearing the twilight of its shelf life. Al tells me that he often visits pubs that they supply to check out the quality of the end product, as this can vary so much depending on the care taken by the landlord. I'm sure if he ever gets too busy to do this there'll be a queue forming to act as 'secret shoppers' on his behalf. We take a stroll over rutted fields in the dark to reach the Beach bar where the Blonde is delivered in its prime. We're running out of beer talk but after a short diversion into football banter I can't resist donning my anorak to indulge in some 'plane talking' with Al. Our techy talk doesn't seem to be boring him too much as we agree to invest in another round, albeit this time buying schooners not pints to add variety to our vessels. I'm almost out of asking all the questions I ever wanted to ask a Tornado pilot and we have agreed on an early start at the brewery the next morning so we bid each other a cheery goodnight and I meander back to my room for a deep sleep.

The combination of the beers, the early hour and the exquisitely comfy bed made it very hard to rise and shine this morning. However, a decent shower and excellent breakfast manage to put a spring back in my step and we're soon making the short journey across town. The brewery looks fresh, clean and new in its modern commercial unit with a separate area for the conditioning tanks and a store of recently filled plastic casks ready for distribution. They also use a lot of half-casks or 'pins' so that pubs that are new to real ales or with low turnover can more easily venture into this brave old world. As Al and Nige don't use cask finings, their beer is conditioned much longer to allow the suspended particles to naturally settle before racking. As a rule of thumb a week of conditioning is allowed for each per cent of alcohol. The clearing of the beer is aided by the highly flocculent strains of yeast adopted for their recipes and the addition of seaweed-based copper finings to the boil. These finings carry a negative electrical charge so that they attract the positively charged proteins, pulling them to the bottom, leaving a clearer, hopped wort behind. Adjacent to all this science, one is also able to appreciate the art of brewing. Hiding under its personal duvet is a barrel of maturing Wolf slowly taking on the flavours of the bourbon and whisky that once occupied the space within.

The brewery was first called West Beach and indeed their casks still bear that name, etched onto their surface. You would think that such a generic name, taken directly from their location, would pose no problems with anyone else's copyright. Remarkably though, a hotel in Bournemouth, without a pennyworth of polite preamble, launched a legal attack insisting that they find another name. This seemed at best unnecessary but the guys were forced to come up with a new name and settled on Windswept, which does neatly convey the nature of the elements in these parts. Sales are predominantly local at this early stage of their evolution and Al half seriously suggests using the Cessna he sometimes flies to deliver beer to a customer just across the Firth, thus saving a long drive around by Inverness. Talking of flying, I am more than a little made up when Al suggests that we go and visit the Tornado simulator housed within the nearby RAF base. We make our way through the light security and soon we're in what looks like a cross between mission control and the best computer game ever. From these screens the trainers can monitor every action of the pilot and create whichever conditions of flight and circumstance that they think may most test his skills. We go through to another room where the copy cockpit (mockpit?) sits high up under a rounded roof on which the surrounding skies will be projected. Al invites me to sit behind the joystick and observe the proliferation of dials, switches and displays around me. Apparently though one should rarely look at these as "anything that can harm you is outside" and therefore you keep your helmet up and manoeuvre based on the information in front of and around you. All too soon we're on our way out of the base and back to

222

Brian where I thank Al profusely for his time and insights into the worlds of brewing and flying. Not many people make IPA in the morning and train RAF pilots in the afternoon.

My next appointment is with David at Spey Valley whose brewery is based within a small building at the back of a farm just a few miles outside Keith. As I guide Brian gently through the mud my eyes notice that it's feeding time in the cowshed, my nose can appreciate the sweet aroma of fresh fertiliser and my Converse are silently praying that I change into my wellies. David is not in the best of spirits today as his plans to try out his new two-barrel brew kit have been stymied by 'someone' forgetting to put the hot water on this morning. This kit replaces his former half-barrel set-up and was procured from the chaps down the road at Loch Ness. We settle down with a coffee in the relative warmth of the 'reception' area used for folk who visit here for hunting, shooting, fishing and other countryside pursuits. There are spent bottles of beer littered around us that may explain why the early call to switch on the water heater was missed this morning. We talk about the thorny subject of the similarly named brewery run by Seb and its previous claim to be the only brewery in Moray. This precipitated the elongated name of David's company 'The Finest Brewery in Speyside Ltd'. He's a busy man as he works full-time in a local distillery while trying to get his beers launched as others begin to crowd the market. There are plans for expansion however to include a new brewery on a new site next to a new house. We have a long chat about the industry and the possible business opportunities therein, such as international distribution, before I return to Brian for the long drive down to Ballater where we shall spend the night.

Our route takes us back through Keith then along narrow roads, twisting past fields and through forest. I brake gently to allow a precious red squirrel to cross the road and see a sign for Dufftown where Homer hopes there will be plenty of his favourite beer. There are signs galore for whisky distilleries, some of which are new to me (the distilleries not the signs), and each pub we pass seems to display old, worn signs for Tennent's and McEwan's – change comes slowly in these parts. I stop off for a macaroni cheese pie thus achieving a hat trick of cheesy pasta meals having had the same for lunch yesterday and a proper plateful served up last night. I make a note to self to try and vary my diet a little more. The roads here make testing demands on Homer's instruction database: "third turning on the right" is followed by "We might find an ice-cream truck, Mmmm, ice cream!" while "third turning on the left" precipitates "Are we there yet?" Half way to Ballater I park up to seek covert, ventilated toilet facilities and make a few calls. I still have no appointments for tomorrow so I chase up Deeside and Brewmeister. The former yields a promise to get someone to call me back as soon as possible, while I manage to speak directly to owner Lewis regarding the latter. It's as well that I called because it turns out they have just moved from their former site near Ballater to Keith, from whence I have just zigged and zagged my way south. There's still time to double back so I coax Brian back into life, complete a neat U-turn and ignore his complaints as we retrace our route.

Homer has pulled us up way short of where we need to be but I eventually manage to locate the new premises that will soon house the expanded brewery of Brewmeister. They're just finishing a tasting with the staff of a pub in Aberdeen that has agreed to sell their beers. This seems like a smart investment of time that will pay off through a loyal frontline sales force. Until the larger brewery is set up they continue to brew on the old kit, looking rather lonely in this relatively cavernous space. They're focussed on bottles only for now and are switching some beers to 330ml from 500ml to better attract their target market; encouraging younger drinkers to break their Stella 'bond' and instead try their stellar Blonde. Brewmeister have already gained a lot of publicity for their Armageddon, which at 65% is being hailed as the strongest beer in the world. They are also experimenting with a malt beer and have produced '10' whose alcohol content I shall leave you to guess. Lewis believes that it will benefit the longer-term marketing and distribution of his range having a name that isn't linked to where the beer is brewed, unlike many smaller breweries. There are also perhaps some similarities here in attitude, style and name to BrewDog - and I suspect in ambition too.

To avoid Brian's tyres treading yet again over the same roads back toward Ballater, I take Lewis's advice on an alternative route that eventually takes us along by the River Dee and dispatches us handily close to the hostel where I shall rest my head tonight. I can also spot the pub he recommended and I later pop in for a refreshing pint of Trade Winds from Cairngorm. After much deliberation on my meal options I plump for the curry house up the road and make my way through a fairly hot dish that breaches my hiccup threshold. I realise, as I drain my glass of house red, that I have failed to garner any appointments for the next day – Deeside haven't responded and I have still to contact Moulin and Strathbraan. I also now have the newly created six°north next to the Marine Hotel in Stonehaven to add to my list, thanks to a tip-off from Al. I need to score at least two breweries the next day to meet my target of six for the week so I sensibly get an early night in preparation for my day of hunting breweries, driving Brian and talking beer to brewers.

The next morning I'm ready to roll but before setting out for the challenging day ahead I need a coffee; ideally a lovely, fresh coffee, served in a cool café that also offers moist, flaky, warm croissants and Wi-Fi. I step out of my hostel in Ballater and walk round to the main street where I am overwhelmed by the incredible choice of such cafes up and down the street, bustling with life and throbbing with customers. Then I hear church bells chiming through the dazzling sunlight and after a few seconds of orientation, I realise I'm still in bed, my alarm reminding me that it's time I debunked. The post shower reality that hits me is the polar opposite of my dream as the only decent looking café I can find doesn't open until 10am. I mean, why would you set up a café that serves coffee then remain closed at the very time of day that people crave your product? My caffeine-free brain tries hard to figure out the best plan for the day ahead and decides to head east via the site of the Deeside Brewery on the way to Stonehaven where I hope I can visit six°north. After a short, muddy detour I fail on the first of these tasks but have to confess to not trying too hard given that my calls have yet to yield any meaningful response and I still haven't had a coffee. As I drive through various towns and villages I'm on the look out for a café that meets my simpler criteria of serving good coffee and being open. As we trundle through Banchory I spy a suitable target, rapidly park up and thoroughly enjoy my delicious reward. I call the Marine Hotel and get an encouraging response that confirms there is a brewery, it's open and someone could show me around. It is with renewed purpose and sharpened senses then that I tune Homer's homing device to the haven of Stones, or Stoney as it is known locally.

The Marine Hotel has come up in conversation with brewers before, mainly due to its Scottish Beer Festival last November where it invited every brewery to submit a cask of ale. Its allegiance to the cause is further demonstrated inside the bar where the walls are festooned with beer mats from virtually every brewery that I've visited. I can also count about six pumps serving up some favourites from around the country with an impressive display of Belgian beer bottles on the shelves above. The owner, Robert Lindsay, is busy but invites me to hang around the bar until he's free – something I have practised many times before in my life. Half an hour later I am ushered upstairs to grab a twenty-minute chat with Robert where I learn that he was once involved with the Houston Brewery but also lived many years in Belgium where he grew to love their beers. Indeed he is currently opening another pub in Aberdeen that will feature a wide choice of these, alongside some of the best brews from this country. Among the Belgian beers will be many from the six°north range that will be brewed in the new premises just up the road. The kit there has a generous 15-barrel capacity and was apparently imported from China although built in the German style. We get onto my favourite topic of kegs versus casks and he suggests that the domination of the former seems an inevitability given the advantages they offer.

I thank Robert for his time, having just dropped in unannounced, and I'm taken up the road to the brewery to meet Michael, a young Austrian who's been appointed to create the, mostly Belgian, beers that will be brewed here. The plant is very new and they've not long finished the test brews ahead of producing their first full commercial runs. Michael has previously worked at Stiegl in Salzburg and spent a year at BrewDog. They won't be using any finings here at all, in the true Belgian style, not even the seaweed-based copper finings that nearly every brewery add to the boil. These beers will clear naturally in the conditioning tanks, helped by the special yeast strains used in the fermentation. Michael tells me that another feature of Belgian beers is that they often have sugar or caramel added with the barley, which I guess helps the ABV reach its often giddying heights. This visit has been as interesting as it was unexpected and I'm intrigued to see how a Scottish brewery making Belgian beers with an Austrian brewer fares against the imported competition and the local, more traditional, creations.

I've got a two-hour drive ahead of me to get to Pitlochry this afternoon in time to visit the Moulin Inn and its brewer, Mike. My call to them had again yielded a result so I'm in buoyant mood as Brian and I set off, secure in the knowledge that my target of six breweries this week will be met. Brian's been working pretty hard these last two days and I'm sure he's been slurping down his oil as well as guzzling his diesel. The drive points us toward Dundee before hanging a right toward the A9 and then up to pretty Pitlochry. The Inn sits about a mile out from town and I'm grateful to be able to give both Brian and I a rest while I munch my sandwich, procured from the garage where Brian's tank was re-filled and my bank balance once again plundered.

I find Mike within the neat wee brewery, occupying what was obviously once a cowshed. The kit is linearly arranged along the back wall, from mash tun to conditioning tanks, with a space for casks to be stored to the front. As I arrive the kettle is gurgling out the last of its alcohol-free juice and sending it on to the adjacent tanks into which, once cooled, the yeast will be pitched to begin its miracle of conversion. Mike brews three times a week and supplies only the hotel next door and its sister, the Atholl Arms. Apparently these keep him pretty busy and last weekend alone there were about 2,000 pints consumed. He describes a rudimentary method he adopts to add some oxygenation to the beer to assist the fermentation – essentially pouring it from a height. I recall Al explaining a similar effect at Windswept but achieved using a pipe that directly injects the gas into the liquid. Every time I think I've heard it all, these brewers come up with something that's new to my limited alcohol acumen. Before I bid Mike farewell, he mentions Strathbraan and asks if I might be swinging past there on my way to Dundee. To be honest I'm tired and my last effort to visit there was spectacularly unsuccessful so I'm not too keen. However, Mike reckons he has the contact details of the brewer, Mark Proctor, and I resolve to snap up the chance to carve another imaginary notch on Brian's non-existent bedpost. As it happens Mike can't locate the details but I've got the scent in my nostrils now so I make my way to the brewery's remote location with the promise of achieving a magnificent seven.

Both Brian and Homer seem to know where they're going and in no time we're parked up once again next to the no parking sign. The place looks every bit as deserted as it did the last time and I'm half tempted to turn around and head for Dundee but, as a veteran brewery hunter, I feel duty bound to press on. Under the notice instructing visitors to ring the bell for attention is another scribbled note explaining that the bell is broken and therefore one should call the given number to alert the family. I do rather feel like I'm intruding but I punch the number into my iPhone only to notice that there's absolutely no signal here. I read the rest of the notice, which offers a 'Plan C' that involves loudly honking your horn. This is all beginning to seem a bit ridiculous but with steely determination I walk the hundred metres back to Brian in order that I may drive him up to the gate so that he may hoot our arrival. A whole minute passes before, to my delight, a figure emerges from within and introductions are made. This is indeed the Mark Proctor whose contact details Mike had been unable to find and he tells me that my timing is spot on as he's been busy all day up until now.

We make our way round by the house, under the gaze of the ten-month old Pointer by the window, and through a garage that has several off-road bikes adorning its interior. The plant here has a capacity of ten barrels but they are only brewing two core beers at the moment, Head East and Due South, taking a measured approach to building their range. The unit that houses the brewery seems tailor made but apparently wasn't created for this purpose. While the present set-up can meet customer demand fairly easily, longer-term plans for expansion of the facility are already in mind. We're indulging in the usual beer chat and have been joined by Mark's dad but I can see that there's work to be done and it's time for me to head to Mum and Dad's for 'tea'; dinner being something you have at lunchtime.

I'm really tired as I drive the short distance to Dundee but elated at having had such a successful day having started with a fairly blank sheet of paper this morning. Indeed it's been a pretty good week all round with the unexpected bonuses of sitting in a Tornado simulator and finding a new brewery that wasn't even on my list. My schedule however is not yet quite complete as I must first pop in to the garage to see if they can perform a transformation on Brian's bodywork. I find Charlie in his office and, despite the rain falling ever harder outside, we take some time to closely inspect Brian in the fading light. There is much oohing, aahing and sucking of air through the teeth so I'm not getting a warm feeling about the prognosis but I am getting wet. We repair to the dry and warmth of Charlie's office, where he can deliver his professional opinion in comfort.

It's no surprise to be told that the previous work done on Brian was sub-standard and that a significant bill would be run up to make him once more pristine. Even then, Charlie continues, the rust would almost certainly return in short order so he suggests I cut my losses and sell, ploughing the cash into a new vehicle. This suggestion is of course like a dagger to my heart. Brian is family – selling him is not an option we would even consider and I'm very glad he was out of earshot when this was said. I politely and calmly ask Charlie for an alternative way forward and he suggests that we just do our best to tend to the rust and keep him roadworthy. It's a reasonable piece of advice but I don't think we're ready to put Brian into palliative care like an ailing geriatric just yet – he's only 25 after all! I thank Charlie for his time and drive off a little sad but resolutely determined to find a solution that will restore Brian to prime condition. How could I even consider doing otherwise after all that we've been through together on this tour?

25 Fancy a Pint?

When I first started to try and get served in a pub I was probably about 16; before then I had to rely on 'carry outs' with the assistance of someone's big brother. I can vividly remember those first few forays into that new and unfamiliar world of the drinking man's den. There was fear of course, both of the unknown and that unfortunate paradox whereby the more you try not to look underage, the more obvious it appears to everyone in the room that you are. The walk from the door to the bar seemed unfeasibly long and the knowing looks from the other punters did nothing to boost my confidence as the moment of truth arrived. When you're afraid your senses become more acute and maybe that's why the nasal cocktail of stale beer, cigarette smoke and body odour has etched itself so permanently into my brain. There aren't many places today that offer such a scintillating smell sensation but if there were, then I'm sure I would be instantly transported back to the dingy dungeon that was the typical 1970s boozer.

In my deepest voice I would nonchalantly demand a pint of heavy/lager/special and get ready to hand over the sweaty coins that had left their imprint on my shaking paw. Refusal wouldn't have been so bad as that would have been over with instantly and made it very clear that I had to exit as fast as possible. Acceptance brought a moment of bliss, a high that was less to do with the delicious brew about to meet my lips and much more about the relief and joy of having been accepted into the midst of this male melee. The worst outcome and, probably the most common, was the excruciating and expert slow torture of the barman's questions as it became entirely clear that he knew you were too young, knew you weren't about to get served but wasn't going to miss the chance to stretch out this morsel of masochism that was punctuating his long, miserable evening.

Having gone to such great lengths to procure a pint, the choices available were often limited to Tennent's Lager, McEwan's Export and Sweetheart Stout. There was not only a complete absence of real ales or craft beers (this was Scotland, worse, Dundee, in the 1970's, remember) but any beers brewed abroad had not even been heard of far less offered for sale. No surprise at all then as I became legally entitled to drink and the eighties bounced into being that the chance to explore the myriad European beers arriving on our shores was a mission I was going to happily accept. CAMRA, to be fair, didn't stand a chance. I don't think I even entertained the thought of real ale and only drank it as a last resort for the best part of the next 25 years. I was probably on the edges of CAMRA's target market but I was resolutely resistant to their charms. I can attribute this to my continuing impression of the hackneyed image of a real ale drinker, the growing range of 'normal' beers readily available wherever I went and the relative paucity of quality real ale pubs in Scotland. Sure, Edinburgh had many pubs that were oases in the desert but I just didn't drink in those kinds of places.

Things did evolve though and the catalysts for me changing were: getting older, letting go of my prejudices, the growing availability of craft beers and moving to London. Had CAMRA failed in taking so long to recruit me to their ranks or was I just slow to pick up on what I was missing? Had they been guilty of being intransigent in their promotion of real ale rather than craft beer or had I just been in the wrong place for too much time? Maybe it was all of the above but when the conversion came it was rapid and I adopted an evangelism typical of the newborn convert. This led me to wonder how many millions more potential converts were yet to find the path and what did that path look like? What were the barriers to them embarking on that journey and what would be the factors that may tempt them? From wine buffs to lager lushes, ladies to laddies and posh birds to punters, how could the real ale or craft beer industry seed and encourage their migration to the other side?

Let's start with the wine buffs. I'm not talking here about just anyone who drinks wine on a regular basis (like me) but those who will actually lay some wine down rather than polish off the two bottles they just bought from Tesco over a weekend. People who can talk knowledgeably about nose, legs, mouth and length without even a snigger while others scoff and quaff. Wine is firmly established as the alcoholic beverage that the middle classes drink with food. Beer is something you have with pies, curries and kebabs. But the world is beginning to change and there are brave first movers out there already, stealing an advantage as they delve into the alternative world of craft beer. Knowing your wines, and the foods they go with, is so last season darling. Already (female) Guardian food critics are extolling the virtues of craft beers, especially as something you'd have to accompany your dinner. Amaze your guests by keeping the cellar door locked and reaching for the key to your ale cabinet. Beers come in an incredible array of styles, strengths, countries of origin and flavours and therefore lend themselves to endless in-depth exploration of taste, texture and smell. Start matching these to food and the permutations are almost infinite, (which I do realise is exactly the same as 'infinite', math dudes). Choose combos that may contrast, complement or cut into the flavours and textures of your chosen dish and just wait for those purrs of satisfaction. Beer is generally less alcoholic than wine and more refreshing but you may wish to serve it in 250ml glasses so that your guests still have room for dessert and don't start singing football songs.

Talking about football, what about your typical lager drinker and their attitude to real ales? The wine buffs may well migrate into drinking lots more craft beer through the medium of the dinner table and the miracle of peer pressure, but that's probably not the route these guys will choose. There are plenty of familiar lager brands that between them offer a fair degree of choice and almost uniform availability, whether in pubs or supermarkets. This is a drinking habit that is easy to maintain and hard to shake off. Many bars, music venues, festivals and corner shops sometimes offer nothing but mass produced global brands so that even the most determined epicure may find themselves indulging with the masses. I think that the likely migration path for these lager-loving birds of a feather involves providing a little bit of what they might fancy in the sort of bar where they might actually meet up with it. Many popular bar chains will offer something for the beer-curious customer who may wish to dabble with the world of ale; possibly something with 'smooth' in its description. Many of these brands are heavily marketed and do a fine job of priming the punter for further research. If that acts as a catalyst to tempt them over toward the other side of the tracks then they really must next find their way out of the bar and into a pub to be able to really start diving into the delectable range of real ales.

Those folk are relatively easy prey as they have a weakness for trying something other than standard lagers. How do we initiate the inveterate lager lush into the world of craft beers? First, they need to be put at risk of accidentally ordering something that looks like a standard lager but is actually a craft beer in disguise. For this to work these must be sold in kegs or perhaps bottles, as many of these bars just wouldn't bother with casks. Next, it needs to be something that isn't too distantly related to a lager but that surreptitiously introduces the unsuspecting drinker into the world of fresh flavours that lie beyond their current perception. I'm not sure that that this brief encounter will necessarily lead to our subject investing in a pipe and joining the Ramblers' Association, but it's a start.

I think we've probably covered most of the glib labels that I had stuck upon our diverse family of drinkers but I would like to spend a little bit of time with the ladies. Ladies may of course fall into either of the categories previously dissected but perhaps we should ask whether the lady beer drinker per se is adequately catered for in our modern world. After all, many other products are designed specifically with the female buyer in mind such as: cars (Honda Fit 'She's'), soft drinks (Diet Coke as opposed to Coke Zero), scented tissues (instead of man-size), even pens (BIC 'For Her') and lots of other stuff that is adapted to be less bulky and more pink. So, what about doing the same with beer? How do ladies' tastes differ in terms of flavour, fizziness, alcohol level, calorific value and even how it's served? I'm sure someone has done some research on this and while I of course recognise that tastes will vary significantly across the female population just as they do for males, I'm quite certain that there will be some differences between the sexes that are not yet being properly catered for. Plus, as The Jam so perfectly suggested, "the public wants what the public gets". Just look at Babycham, alcopops, shots that taste like medicine and even alcoholic energy drinks.

Finding something new that may appeal to discerning female drinkers may depend on how it's presented as much as what it actually is. Given the range of beer styles that already exist I don't think we need a bunch of chemists and brewers locked up in a laboratory for 6 months to figure this out. I, for one, am willing to engage in extensive market research that will involve long hours of drinking with ladies in order to ascertain their preferences and give them exactly what they want. Light beers, low fizz beers or fruity beers, served up in flutes, champagne saucers or even a snifter. This may prove to be one of the last undiscovered destinations in the universe of beer. Except, of course, it isn't. Carlsberg have already launched two beers aimed at the ladies – Copenhagen and Eve. Molson Coors tried one called

Animee but it was withdrawn because of poor sales. There's even one in America called Chick Beer, which must rate as one of the worst names ever. So some have tried and none have yet succeeded in any big way. Is it a dead end idea or is it just that no one has got it right yet? I think I'd probably vote for the former.

One matter that would have to be addressed is the name that we'd give to our lady-beers. There must be something approaching 10,000 different beer products in the UK, all with their own name. The most interesting ones are those that have recently emerged from the craft beer/real ale world. These are often very traditional in their nature or perhaps have some link to history. Many are weird and wonderful but unless you know the story behind them, their origins will remain a mystery. Many of them involve puns, most of which are quite risible. Cool names would attract me to give those ales a try while naff ones would put me off upfront so these things do matter.

I've become guilty of peering at beer clips in pubs, bent over with screwed-up eyes, scrutinising all the details while the barman waits patiently for my order. What I'm looking for is a description of the beer, its ingredients, alcohol content and even a wee story about its origins. Great barmen can talk you through all of this, decent barmen will let you try for yourself but some just go and serve another customer. In the absence of such detail then the name and the branding are often all you have to go on when deciding which pump to plump for. Some of my favourite beer names in Scotland include Simmer Dim, Happy Chappy, Berserker, Schiehallion and Tactical Nuclear

Penguin. But what if we were to design a range just for the ladies? The brewery could be called 'Fem' Ales perhaps? Some of the core beers might be named Goddess Lager, Raspberry Redhead or Aphrodite Ale? I can recommend creating beer names, for either or both genders, as an excellent topic of conversation next time you're having a few drinks with friends.

So, beer has come a long way from basic un-hopped ales, the role of the brewster, the growth of major breweries in the 19th century and the advent of international distribution through India Pale Ales. Independent brewers seemed to fall away as the 20th century progressed and a few major brands dominated for much of the next several decades. Then came the international brands, global marketing and the ability to drink certain beers anywhere in the world and to travel extensively trying new beers in every country you visit. Enjoying real ale had become a niche pastime and independent brewers were clinging on to a tiny proportion of the market. Then sometime around 1990 a change started to happen and a new world of microbreweries was born. In Scotland for example there may have been not more than a dozen breweries in the early 90s but now they number nearly 70 and counting. CAMRA reported record numbers of new breweries starting up around the UK in recent years, with over 150 in one year alone. This brings the total in the UK to over 1000 breweries. We see growth in real ale and craft beers being around 5-10% while beer sales are generally falling as people migrate to wine and pubs are closing as people choose to drink at home.

So, where now for the future of beer? We've never had so much choice in what we drink and where we drink it. The mass produced brands may change ownership now and again but they are surely here to stay. Any growing, mid-sized brewing company that hasn't already been gobbled up is going to need strong defences to resist offers from the big players when these come around. You've got to expect similar consolidation further down the food chain and there will no doubt be casualties among the very small players unless they have a solid niche to hide within. I guess what I'm saying is that we should make hay while the sun shines. Drink beer while the barley grows. We have possibly never had it so good and a world of incredible tastes, smells and flavours await us all. Exploring new pubs and trying new beers is a lot of fun. Having the chance to drive around Scotland visiting most of the breweries therein, meeting the brewers and sampling their beers was fabulous fun. Learning about beer and the brewing industry was an education. Discovering beer in the land of whisky with my friend Brian was a privilege and a joy. I do hope that reading about it all has been a pleasure for you too. We're not finished yet though...

26 Hitting Sixty

One of the challenges along this journey has been identifying the existing, and keeping up with the new, breweries in Scotland. I have no doubt at all that, as I write this, there will be a small number of brewers covertly preparing their preliminary pints before announcing their arrival on to this crowded stage. As I near the conclusion of my field research I can more confidently assess the state of play. I have thus far visited 56 breweries. A visit only counts if I see round the brewery and meet the brewer or another member of staff. At this moment in time there are 68 breweries on my list, which includes the Angus Brewery that has unfortunately ceased to exist since my visit. I have excluded cuckoo brewers as they don't have a brewery to show off and Tennent's because…well, just because. I have failed to see Madcap, BrewDog and Deeside and it's unlikely that I shall have the opportunity to knock on any of their doors again any time soon. Madcap was just bad timing, BrewDog insisted that they really weren't set up for visitors and Deeside seemed unwilling or unable to respond to the messages I left.

My target now is to complete sixty breweries excluding Caledonian and Belhaven. I have no problem with either of these players but it doesn't feel right to rely upon paying upwards of a tenner to take a standard tour around breweries that are far from being independent, in order to achieve my target. This leaves me with two newbies, Beeches and Archerfield; two that I have failed with before, Williams and TSA; Loch Leven that I couldn't previously find, Fyfe that seems not to be in operation presently and Arran that I had to abandon due to inclement weather. So there are 66 excluding Caledonian and Belhaven, leaving ten that I have not seen of which there are three I won't see and one (Fyfe) I probably can't see. This means that I have to score four visits from the remaining six viable targets to meet my diamond anniversary target. With Williams and TSA looking like outsiders, I pretty much have my four final prey identified: Beeches and Loch Leven in Fife, Archerfield east of Edinburgh and Arran, way out west. Achieving sixty visits would be beyond my earlier, more pessimistic estimates and would feel like a real achievement, but there's still work to be done.

The long train journey north eventually takes me across the Forth and Tay bridges and delivers me safely to Dundee. As I exit the station I am presented with a fine view of the Discovery, its many masts standing tall and proud, before hopping in a waiting taxi up to my parents' place. Brian's looking cleaner than when I left him thanks to some torrential rain and hopefully he's feeling perky ahead of a demanding day tomorrow. Our plans involve visiting three breweries, driving almost two hundred miles and catching a ferry, all within a ten-hour window. After a nut loaf and my second alcohol-free evening on the trot, I sleep well and rise early to load Brian up and program Homer for Lochgelly, where we shall be dropping in to see Beeches Brewery, one of the many recent start-ups in Scotland.

The brewery is named after the Brookside-like cul-de-sac where the owner Kenny lives and where he maintains his nano-kit in a small garage out the back. I had been assuming that the vessels adjacent to where we were chatting had to be his test kit but when I enquire after the location of the actual brewery Kenny confirms, "you're standing in front of it". I've seen some pretty small breweries during this tour but it looks very much like Kenny will be awarded the honour of having the smallest commercial brewery in Scotland. I'll have to check my notes to confirm this prestigious award of course but at a scale of only ten gallons (the size of a Texan's hat), each brew is sufficient only to fill one cask. He brews three times a week but demand is increasing so he plans to add another fermenter soon to increase total capacity. There are no conditioning tanks so he simply racks from the fermenters once the beer has cooled and leaves the casks (often pins rather than firkins) for about three weeks before sending them on to customers.

Kenny's just back from a beer festival at Loch Ness and is also busy sending more casks to festivals as far away as Barnsley, through a connection with Bob Phaff at St Andrews. There seems to be quite a brotherhood among the neighbouring brewers, with Tryst also sending a cask for Kenny to fill for another festival. It's almost time for me to set off for my next brewery so I tell Kenny that I'm heading next for Loch Leven. At this, he offers directions, pointing across some fields towards Kelty in the distance, just beyond which lies my target, in the tiny village (aka row of houses) of Maryburgh. Brian's been busy chatting to the campervan I parked him next to in Kenny's drive, no doubt comparing travel itineraries and telling humorous stories about their respective human owners. I interrupt their imaginary discussion, carefully reverse back out and guide my trusty friend toward our next engagement.

Having not managed to locate the Loch Leven Brewery last time around, I'm grateful for Kenny's local knowledge, advising me to look for the first house on the right. Neil answers the door and we're soon inspecting his four-barrel kit, which is situated at the back of his property. Although Neil has about fifteen times the capacity of Kenny he only brews a couple of times a month so his total production isn't significantly larger. The inside walls look freshly painted but apparently these were done years ago using a very expensive paint, typically found in operating theatres, which doesn't allow any bacteria or nasty infections to take root. This is important as these air-born baddies can easily find their way into your kit, especially the intricate micro-highways of the heat exchanger. Chatting away with brewers like this has now become second nature to me thanks to a) a growing knowledge and interest, b) a lot of practice and c) an improving 'brewside' manner that hopefully puts folk at ease with this wandering stranger. My conservative nature is quietly prompting me to once again move on so as not to risk missing the all-important ferry trip tonight. I thank Neil for his time and re-enter the comfort zone that is Brian's cockpit. In no time we're crossing the Forth road bridge heading south, looking over at the rail bridge that yesterday we crossed heading north, looking over here.

As we make our way through East Lothian I'm looking around in vain for somewhere that may offer a decent coffee. Gullane, with its posh shops, commuter residents and golf course, seems to be the primary candidate but the brewery's only another five minutes' drive so I decide to recce there first. I pull up in front of the big iron gates next to the sign advertising that the Archerfield Walled Garden, home of the brewery, is now open. The gates are decidedly closed though and there appears to be absolutely no life within. I'm extremely puzzled as I'm obviously in the right place but even approaching the gates in the hope of a hidden sensor yields no movement. I return to Gullane for a coffee and, brain function restored, decide that there must be another gate further on. This proves correct and after parking Brian I enter the grand visitor centre, bar and restaurant. The brewery lies to the left, clearly visible through the glass, and I am taken aback by the sheer scale of it. I had imagined a modest, simple, five-barrel creation but this is a serious, shiny, salubrious set-up in a space about the size of a 7-a-side football pitch. The last time I'd talked to Robert Knops he was cuckoo brewing through TSA and indicating that he may be sorted out with his own place by March. Well, he's certainly achieved that and he's presently striding over to greet me and say hello.

It turns out that Robert is a Heriot-Watt alumnus, having been there around the same time as Steve Stewart of Stewart Brewing fame. He has since worked at a few of the larger brewers such as Guinness, Whitbread and Coors before going it alone. The tour that follows is as interesting as it is in-depth and I do my very best to keep up. Like Cromarty (if I recall correctly) he uses a mash conversion vessel and lauter tun rather than just the traditional mash tun. The temperature of the mash can be controlled and altered using a steam jacket that takes the liquid up in stages from 45° to 78° before it transfers to the lauter tun where it's raked then sparged. It's then sent back to the mash conversion vessel, which doubles up as a copper and has a clever device at the bottom that creates a whirlpool to leave behind the trub, including the spent particles from the hop pellets. I'm surprised about the pellets but Robert reckons these are good for imparting bitterness, even if arguably less effective for aroma. I haven't seen anything quite like this kit before, with its outsized hopback, two-stage heat exchanger and integral oxygenation device. The scale overall is 'only' 11 barrels but there are plenty of conditioning tanks to store the beer until demand requires it to be sent on its way, mostly in casks, to customers located within a fifty-mile radius or so. On top of (not literally) all of this impressive production line is a state of the art bottling line, presently lying silent but capable of filling, capping and labelling about a thousand bottles an hour with robotic precision.

I'm in need of a drink now and Robert obliges by drawing me a taster of his California Common from one of the tanks. It's delicious and I sip away as he takes me outside to see the large space that is being slowly transformed into the key attraction at Archerfield, the Victorian walled garden. I'm hoping that the obvious connection is made and that one day we have a fully functioning Victorian walled *beer* garden to complement the tours that Robert will shortly be providing to a curious and thirsty public.

It's been a fairly windy day thus far, which sows a seed of doubt in my mind regarding the likelihood that my 6 o'clock ferry will sail. I really don't want to write off another hotel room and don't fancy a night in Ardrossan (it's not a bad place but does contain 'dross') but the sea is surprisingly calm and we make an easy, on-time crossing to Brodick. I soon arrive at the hotel and check in at the compact bar, brim-full of elderly diners. There isn't a seat to be had but I am assured by my host Trev, as he shows me to my room, that they will have all cleared off by the time the pop quiz starts at 9pm. I'd eaten on the ferry so make my evening entrance a bit later than usual, timed to be able to neck a pint of the Arran Blonde ahead of the anticipated quiz. I follow this up with Peter's Well from the Houston Brewery and enter into some amiable chat with a couple of locals and an Aussie called Bryce (presumably a posh version of 'Bruce'). I'm invited to join their quiz team and after a short delay Trev appears from nowhere, resplendent in a gold, sequinned jacket, ready to test us with forty questions and fifteen intros. I'm little better than useless but the local lads, Lenny and Ian, inspire us to a respectable 43 and a half points, finishing second from a field of four. The winners are a team of two whose prize is a free drink each. It strikes me that large teams would pay dividends here both in terms of points and prizes!

The next day I've got a few hours to kill before the Arran Brewery tour starts at 2pm and the weather is behaving so I take a walk by the shore before ascending half way up towards Goat Fell. I swing around by the castle and grab a sarnie that I munch back by the sea front as I watch the ferry plough its watery course. Those few hours have now been put to rest and it's time to experience my sixtieth brewery, housed in what was once the castle laundry room. There's a decent-sized shop as you enter, shelves groaning under the wide range of bottled beer and touristy trinkets. I'm saved from being the sole soul on this tour by an English couple and we are soon beckoned through to the brewery beyond. There are four small televisions attached to the walls, spread out along the length of the narrow passage, separated from the brewery by a glass partition. I imagine that these will all show the same video simultaneously, enabling larger crowds to enjoy a syncopated education session. Instead, the presentation comes in four separate parts and we move along in unison so that each section, presented by bearded boss Gerald Michaluk, occurs adjacent to the relevant piece of brewing kit. Despite the cheesy Scottish music that closes each section, it's a pretty thorough and enjoyable effort, complemented by large cartoon illustrations, information boards and even a glossary on the surrounding walls. Back in the main shop we are treated to a rapid-fire tasting of six of their beers. I think I'm making decent progress as we hang on to this speeding beer train but the other bloke is necking the next one before I've demolished the previous one. At £4 it's not by any means an expensive tour but pales in comparison to others like Archerfield where the tour is free, personal and I'm usually sent on my way with an armful of freebie beer. I do feel a little emotional with this being my sixtieth and last brewery so to mark the occasion I purchase a Red Squirrel ale that reminds me of the label I imagined for the ale I brewed, all those months ago, with Douglas at Tin Pot. After a pleasant chat with the young lady in the shop I'm off to board the ferry and pick up Brian for his final journey in his official capacity of Tour Vehicle.

So, what started on Shetland has ended on Arran. Quite by accident, having started on our most northerly island, I have finished, appropriately, on our most southerly (not counting the uninhabited Ailsa Craig – famous for providing the raw material for curling stones – and Sanda, which is privately owned). I have been to some stunningly beautiful locations and Brian has taken us through some of Scotland's loveliest scenery. There can be few industries more diverse or dispersed than brewing in Scotland. The variations in scale, style, age, ambition and character are quite spectacular – and that's just the brewers, never mind the breweries! We have covered all points on the compass, flirting with the border at Kelso and Annan, visiting seven islands (six of which I'd never been to before) by road, ferry and plane and zig-zagging our way across pretty much all of this gorgeous country, usually via one of Homer's 'scenic' routes. That Sunday morning in Islington when I set out for the long journey to Unst, I was naively aiming to visit every brewery in Scotland. Half way through this book I was beginning to feel content with a target of fifty but a record breaking week in Moray and Aberdeenshire gave us the turbo boost we needed to achieve the magic sixty.

27 I Missed You

I couldn't bring closure to this book without proper mention of the nine (including Tennent's) Scottish breweries that I didn't manage to see and also one other that I have yet to mention, but which I fully intend to visit at some future date. I think I've now found peace with the reality of not ticking every box and satisfaction with having seen so many. I was sorry not to be able to meet John at Madcap in Annan but he was heading off for a couple of weeks' well-earned holiday when I was in his neck of the woods. I guess I could have swapped Annan for Arran in hitting sixty but I couldn't resist the allure of another island. John's beers apparently spend at least three months conditioning in the cask or tank and some of his specialty brews can mature for up to eighteen months, so I'm hoping to make it back there some day for a tasting. As for Fyfe Brewery, I did kind of visit that one and would have happily returned but all indications were that they weren't brewing anymore and may even have been looking to sell the kit from what I heard on the grapevine (hopbine?). If I ever find myself in Kirkcaldy during opening hours though, I'll pop in and find out what they're up to. I was disappointed not to hear back from Deeside as I could easily have popped in on my way to Stonehaven that day. They may just have been too busy to call back or perhaps don't really welcome visitors but in any case I had to write that one off.

I think my greatest disappointment was not being able to visit Williams Bros. They are a significant player in the Scottish craft beer market, they create the un-hopped Fraoch Heather Ale within their range and Scott Williams was a name that came up frequently when talking with brewers. It was disappointing also because I did get pretty close and there remains a feeling that perhaps I should just have turned up; sometimes it's better to ask for forgiveness than permission! Traditional Scottish Ales (TSA) was not so much the one that got away but rather the one I didn't fish very hard for to start with. I can't really explain why but I got the distinct impression that this was more of a manufacturing plant, making beer as much for others as themselves and that a warm welcome may not have been forthcoming. I did try to make contact on a couple of occasions, but I just didn't try all that hard. When it comes to not trying though, the biggest gap in my communications effort was definitely Tennent's. To tell you the truth, I felt that this household name was an entirely different breed to the prey that I was seeking and it never even crossed my mind to contact them. They may also be the only brewery in Scotland whose beers I would flat-out refuse to drink. On top of that I did learn at one point that unless you were connected to the industry (I still see myself as an outsider of course) you wouldn't be able to gain entry anyway. So, I definitely don't have too many regrets on that one.

As I mentioned earlier, I would not have hesitated to visit Caledonian or Belhaven if I had run out of other options while still a brewery or two short of hitting my target of sixty. My reticence to give these two old breweries priority on my list comes about partly because they are now owned by very large concerns outside of Scotland i.e. Heineken and Greene King respectively. The other reason, however, was simply that I didn't think there would be much to discover that I couldn't find out online and their standard, if no doubt professional, tour would be unlikely to yield vast additional knowledge for me or copy for this book. That said, I do feel a wee pang of guilt and plan to make time to visit both during future trips to Scotland – I might then have to eat my words. Caledonian is easy as it's in central Edinburgh and, while Belhaven is out at Dunbar on the coast, they did sponsor Dundee United for six years so I guess I owe them one. Meantime, interested readers can discover all about their history (the breweries, not the football team) with just a few clicks. I've got to say that the Caledonian website is much the superior of the two, offering greater historic and personal insights.

That leaves me with BrewDog. On their website is the statement "BrewDog is a post Punk apocalyptic mother fu*ker of a craft brewery". Really? Well, as brand definitions go it's certainly straight to the point, uncompromising and edgy; a description that could as easily be applied to much of their marketing and indeed their range of beers. ('Arrogant' was another adjective that I heard used to describe them on occasion but I'm not sure they wouldn't take that as a compliment!) Ever since they came on the scene, bursting through the yawning gap between real ale and mass-produced lagers, they have been creative and distinctive in just about everything they've done. (Driving a tank up London's Camden High Street must qualify as one of the more striking and memorable marketing stunts ever pulled.)

That has in turn led to spectacular growth and an impact on the customer that means that even if you don't drink their beers, you know who they are; not least due to their growing number of strategically placed bars. As they say themselves "Welcome to the Craft Beer Revolution". Unfortunately they didn't say 'welcome' to me and therefore I can add nothing more to all the stuff you can find out for yourself online.

If I had managed to visit these last nine breweries then, not only would this book have been longer (and maybe richer), it would also have required a gestation period beyond the (appropriately human) nine months I have afforded it. Had I managed to gain entry to these last nine breweries, I would also have reached the giddy heights of 69 visits and would then be looking around feverishly for number seventy. Actually, I do know exactly which brewery would have had that honour and it would have taken me all the way back to Shetland where we started, but this time to the capital Lerwick and their brand new, eponymous brewing company. As of today the website is tantalising us with a message that "more than excitement is brewing" and a suggestion that we can look forward to some 'Shetlandic' beers. For me, a visit back to Shetland would be a fabulous postscript to this book and the journey that gave birth to it. It wasn't just that Shetland was the scene of my virgin visit to a brewery or that it provided the experience of exploring Unst, Britain's most northerly island. Despite tough competition from most of the islands and many of the places I visited, it stands out as the most memorable and special experience of my whole trip. And oh, that accent!

28 Brian Comes Home

'Life with Brian' has so far involved three amazing adventures. The first took us through Eastern Europe and a steep learning curve about how to look after a campervan and survive life in a campsite. With our rookie status behind us, we were then able to relax and enjoy three months in Western Europe, despite dodgy electrics and being one turbo short of a proper engine. This latest adventure, which you have now shared, has also been very special but quite different.

Visiting sixty breweries in a country famed for distilleries in a Dutch van between autumn and spring means that I've been seeking the 'wrong' drink, on the 'wrong' side of the road at the 'wrong' time of year; but it felt so right! I've done it (more or less) alone, often resorting to imaginary conversations with just an old van (and an eccentric navigation device) for company. I've deserted him every weekend, hibernated him for three months, driven him in some awful conditions and frequently stretched his performance limits, but he's never let me down – quite an achievement for a van of his age. Indeed, in honour of his faithful service, it is my intention to publish this book on or near to his 25th birthday - 29th June 2013. If he is to enjoy a long and happy retirement then our Brian is in need of some serious attention and lots of tender, loving care. I'm sure that by this stage of the book you have also developed a remote affection for this old soldier of the road (him, not me) and won't be able to rest without knowing that he will be properly looked after and cared for in his old age. Let me put your mind at rest dear reader as, despite strong protestations from my pocket, we will be investing in his long-term wellbeing just as soon as we get him back down to London, his tour of duty complete. To that end I am making one last official journey to Scotland to pick him up, clean him up and cheer him up with confirmation of his demob papers and imminent early retirement.

While I've been away, Brian's been catching up on his sleep, parked up safe and secure down a quiet residential street on Edinburgh's Southside. As well as being entirely free of cost, this arrangement is quite flexible, so I decide to let him rest a little longer while I spend the afternoon playing snooker with my son, Nick. My plan is to drive to Sheffield this Saturday and stay the night with friends before completing Brian's triumphant return to London, 224 days (or 32 weeks) after we first set off. Before then, Brian kindly helps us out with some recycling and shopping, as well as taking a mate to lunch and friends to dinner. Saturday morning soon arrives and brings some welcome sunshine with it for the drive south. I think we're both looking forward to going home knowing that we've achieved our goal in Scotland, but Brian does choke up a little when we cross the border back into England. I push his choke back down and soon we're joining the longest road in the country, the A1, for the landmark journey ahead.

After a night of excellent beer and curry in Sheffield, where Jo has been happily reunited with Brian, we set off for what should be an unremarkable drive to London. Our first priority is to refill Brian's fuel tank that was completely emptied by the journey from Edinburgh – 10k to the litre is not a formula for infrequent filling. There's a whiff of petrol in the air as we exit the steel town, which we attribute to some source outside of Brian and plough merrily on. After we refuel though, the smell intensifies, as do our concerns, and we realise that what we're smelling isn't someone else's petrol, it's Brian's diesel! We pull in to the next service station, which luckily lurks only a few miles down the road. We clamber out and rush to Brian's rear end where we can see smoke coming out, which we know not to be a good sign! In my panic I forget that he has a fire extinguisher inside and go to ask the garage for one. Meantime we call for assistance and hope that we aren't about to see Brian engulfed in flames, an ignominious end to his illustrious career. I admonish myself for momentarily thinking of the silver lining that at least we won't have to make all those repairs now.

The smoke is easing up a little so we're downgrading our diagnosis from terminal to treatable, but we will have to wait a couple of hours before help arrives and a proper assessment can be made. My main concern has now turned to how I get 27 bottles of beer back home if we have to leave Brian at a garage somewhere near Chesterfield for repairs. I have invited a bunch of mates round this Friday to celebrate Brian's return by consuming all the beers I accumulated on the tour, net of those ones that have already been imbibed or given away. Not wishing to let them down, I start filling up my backpack, daypack and a smelly old shopping bag with my booty, ready to drag onto the train home. This feels a bit like carrying a stricken marathon runner over the line just to get the medal, given that Brian has carried this weight for months now, but needs must. When help arrives the diagnosis is as rapid as it is welcome. It seems that the small diesel leak-off pipe has become detached so that fuel is spilling over the engine – hence the smell and the smoke. Luckily the mechanic has a spare part and in no time we are ready to complete our journey, Brian is back to normal and the beer will arrive safely. Hoorah!

Having looked disaster in the eye and made our escape without any great fuss or expense, there's a positive mood glowing within Brian. This tiny bubble of effervescence gains some more fizz as we spot two or three other Brians speeding along the opposite carriageway and mutually admiring waves of kinship are exchanged. To our amazement we then see a few more and in no time the count is into double figures. Within half an hour dozens have zoomed past and soon our arms are aching from constant, excited greetings. This procession of classic camping vehicles can only be explained by there having been some kind of gathering of enthusiasts further south, but the timing of this parade is propitious. To Brian, this is a welcoming party, a guard of honour, a celebratory drive-past by his peers in recognition of his achievements. After months of hard work and near disaster just minutes before, this is a serendipitous show of support for the homecoming hero. I can detect a purr to his engine note, a lightness in his suspension and maybe just a moistening of his wiper jets. Brian's coming home.

I spend the final part of our drive thinking about the fun we're going to have now that Brian's not busy with work. Soon, we're off to Switzerland for a couple of weeks to rediscover the joys of camping and driving on the right side of the road. We've got two music festivals lined up, safe in the knowledge that we can retreat to Brian's relatively warm and capacious interior, while others brave the cold and rain in their flimsy tents. Tomorrow he shall take us to an eightieth birthday party, showing off his practical value as well as his leisure credentials. Many other trips will follow but before then we have to dig deep and invest in his vital organs, skin problems and general wellbeing. Many well-meaning people have suggested, with a serious frown, that we would be better to trade him in and get a new one. That would be anathema and we would rather do everything we can to extend his life, whatever the price, and live with the consequences than find ourselves with a changeling while he's at the mercy of a new owner or, worse, a scrapyard.

Soon after returning home we receive the shocking news that Brian doesn't comply with the London Low Emission Zone requirements, due to being a big, old diesel van that belches smoke every time he starts. This is really bad news but he's been caught on camera and the pollution police have given us a month to find a solution. We're definitely not going to pay the £100 daily charge to use him around town and the cost of fitting an exhaust filter almost matches his total value so we are left with only the third option…put him out to pasture.

What this means in practical terms is that we pay to have him stored off road, fifty miles away in Essex. This is a fairly financially neutral solution but less than convenient as we will have to transport luggage and bikes on the train every time we want to take him out. On the other hand however it seems quite fitting that he will spend most of his semi-retirement in the company of his peers, able to exchange stories of travel and adventure, while comparing the litany of mechanical aches and pains that have been suffered along the way. He'll be comfortable, safe and warm under his faithful onesie and we shall of course visit as often as possible to take him for a spin. All the same, I know I'm going to really miss being able to look out of my window each morning to see the familiar, sludge-brown shape of my old friend Brian, slumbering in the sun and dreaming of our happy days together, discovering beer in the land of whisky.

These 27 beers, brought home by Brian,

were consumed at the end of tour party

Thanks and Contact

The process of creating this book was often fun, sometimes challenging but always educational. Bringing it to life has only been possible through the support and input of many people. Big hugs to:

Greg, Steve and Soapy for joining me on the trip

Joan, Mark and Kevin for their valuable editorial feedback

Mum, Dad and Nick for having me stay

Dave for his excellent publishing tips

Friends and family for their help in choosing the best cover image

Special thanks to all those folk I met across sixty breweries without whose kindness this book could not have been written and to Brian and Homer for being my constant companions.

And finally, love and hugs to Jo for giving me the support I needed and letting me go play with Brian for a few months!

Thank you also for reading this book – I hope you enjoyed it! Please visit my website to say hi, maybe leave some comments and catch up on any future adventures. Cheers!

www.bobbyorbit.com

@bobbyorbit

Photo courtesy of Steve Bainbridge

ABOUT THE AUTHOR

After 26 years in the high-octane world of occupational pensions, Robert decided he had to escape and try something new. He packed his backpack, spent two years traveling the world with Jo and started to keep a blog of their adventures. Once back home in London he couldn't face wearing a suit again so decided to continue to travel and write.

The Tea Leaf Paradox is his first book and the inspiration for wanting to start his own brewery. Robert lives in Camden Town, London, with his partner Jo and has a son, Nick, in Edinburgh

Printed in Great Britain
by Amazon.co.uk, Ltd.,
Marston Gate.